FLAMINGO FANDANGO
AND OTHER
PICTURES IN COLOR

Other Books by Eric Felderman

The Riddle of the Universe Solved! (With 37 Misleading Pictures)

The Sins of Santa Claus   (Illustrated)

Vain Bibble Babble

Shakespeare Corrected and Improved

Ecclesiastes Variations

Strange Events Coloring Book

Dream Diary

(and others)

Selections read on You Tube

FLAMINGO FANDANGO
AND OTHER
PICTURES IN COLOR

by

Eric Felderman

KDP

Copyright © by Eric Felderman 2024

All Rights Reserved

Cover by Eric Felderman

ericfelderman23@yahoo.com

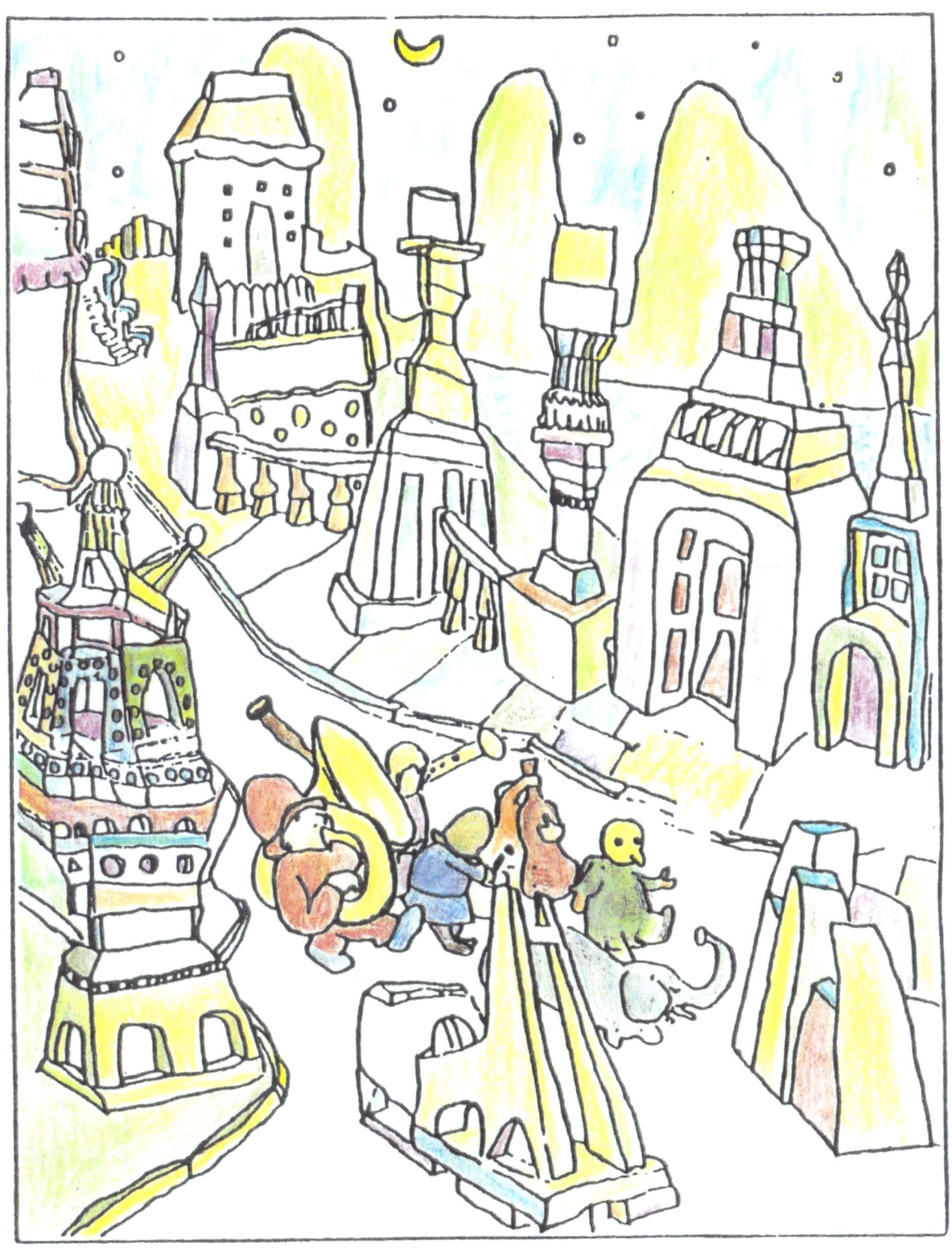

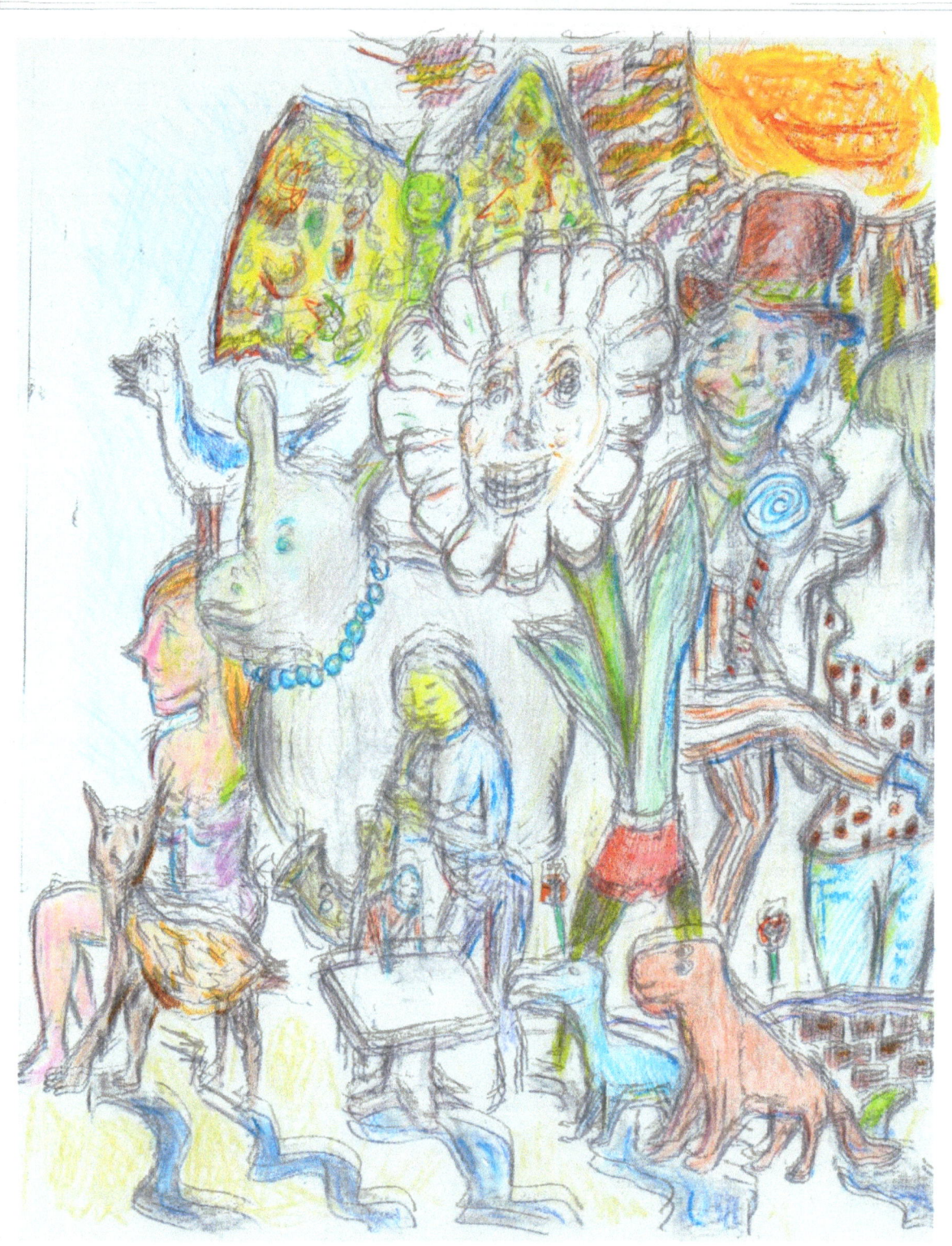

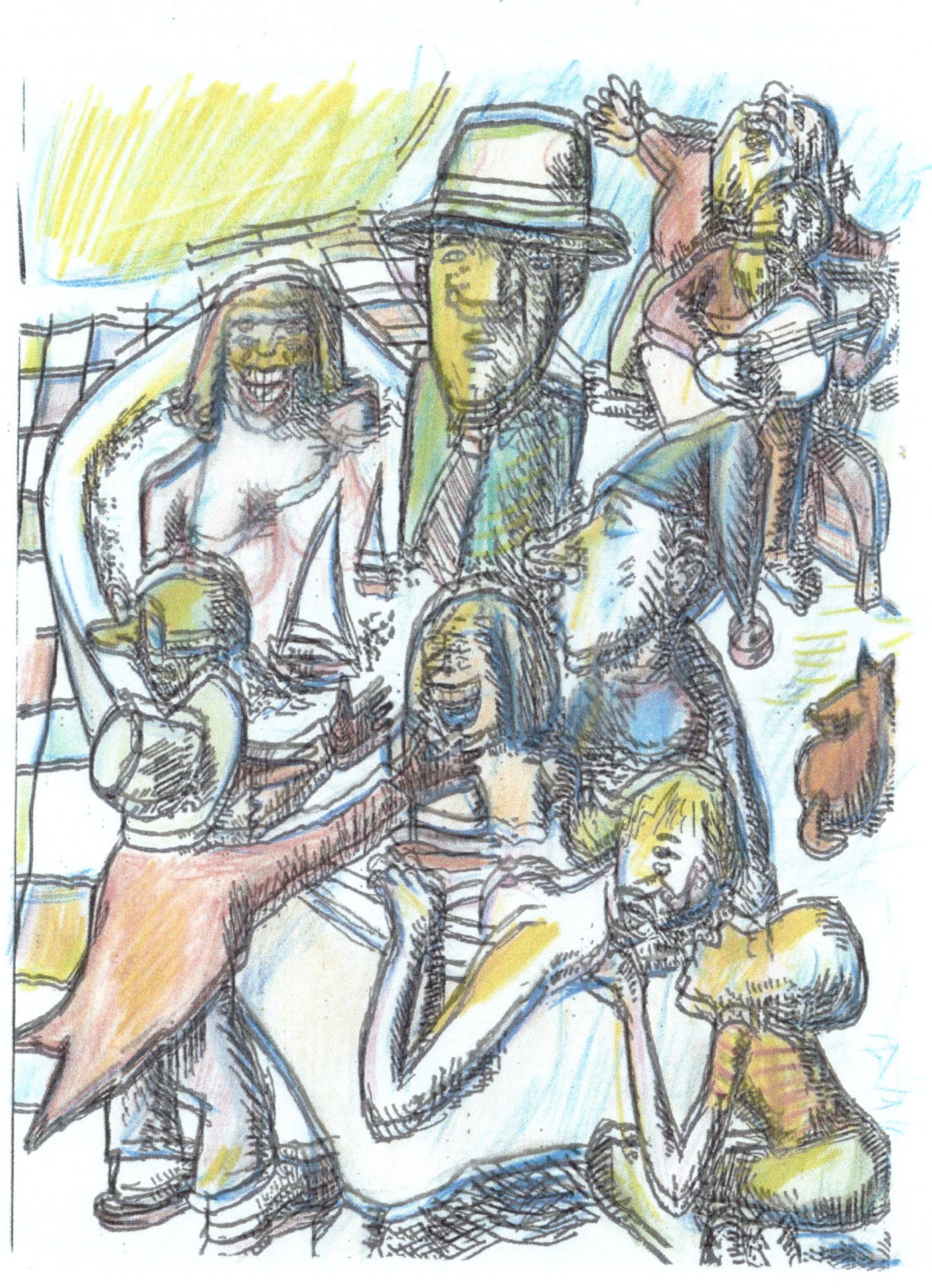

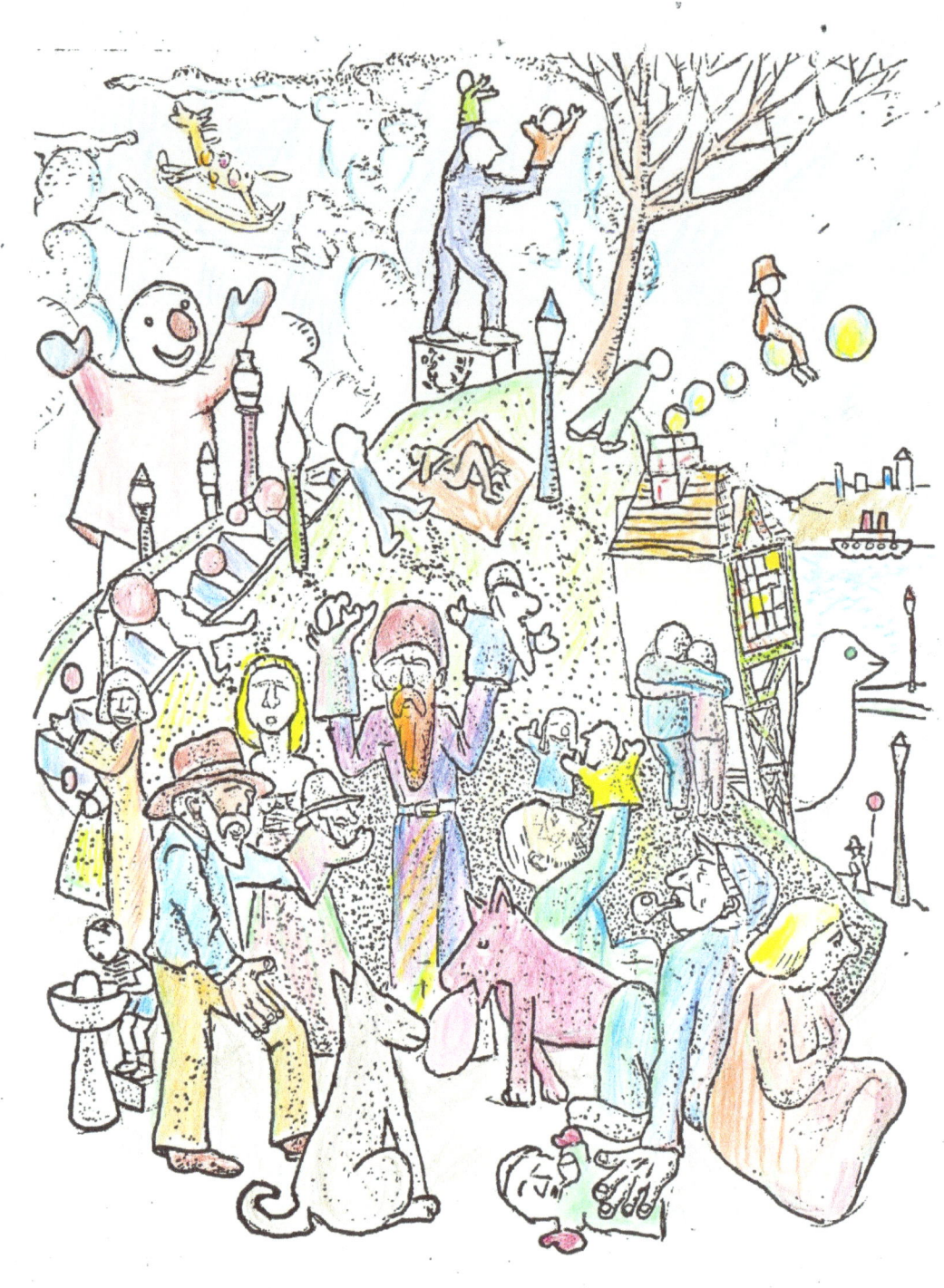

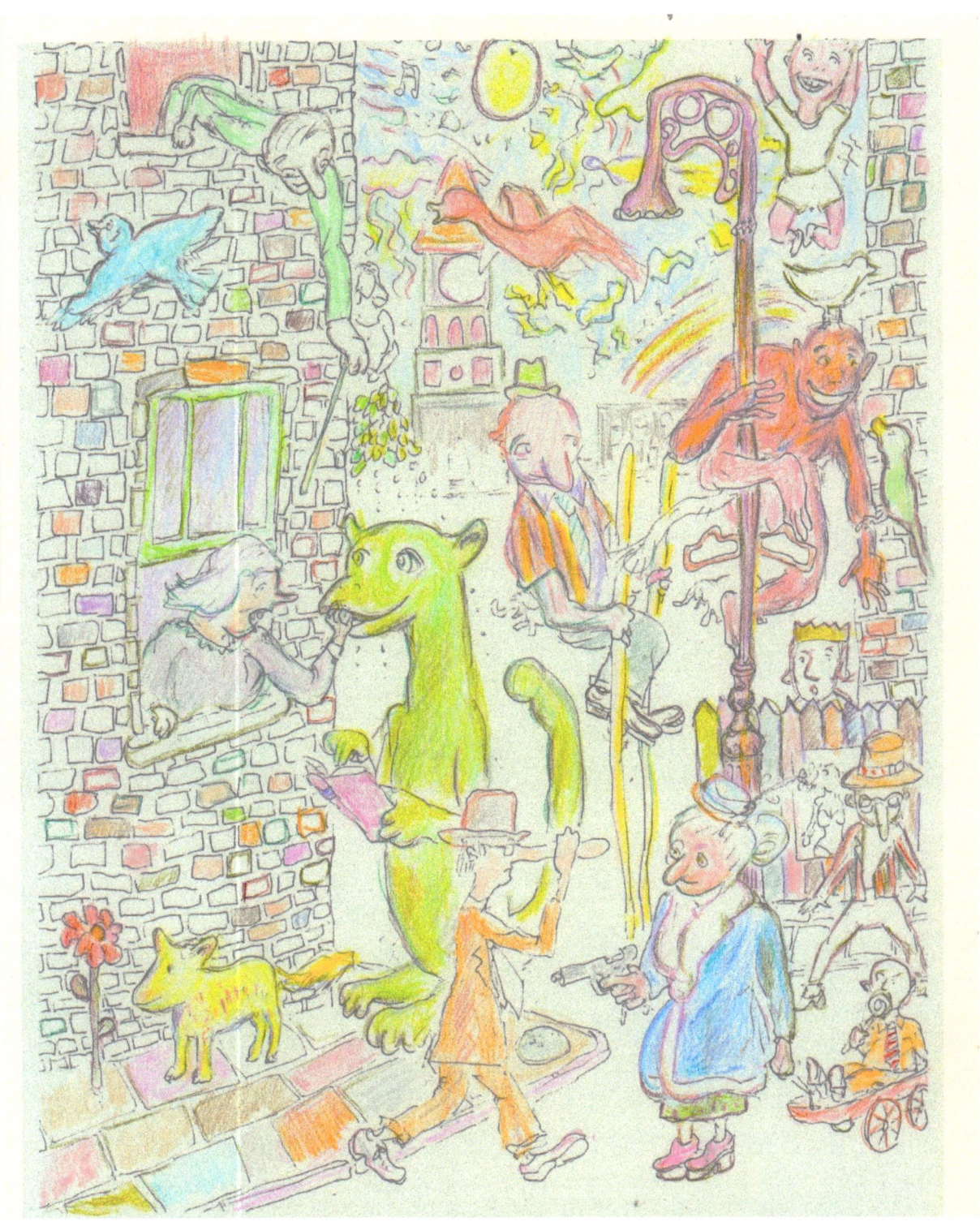

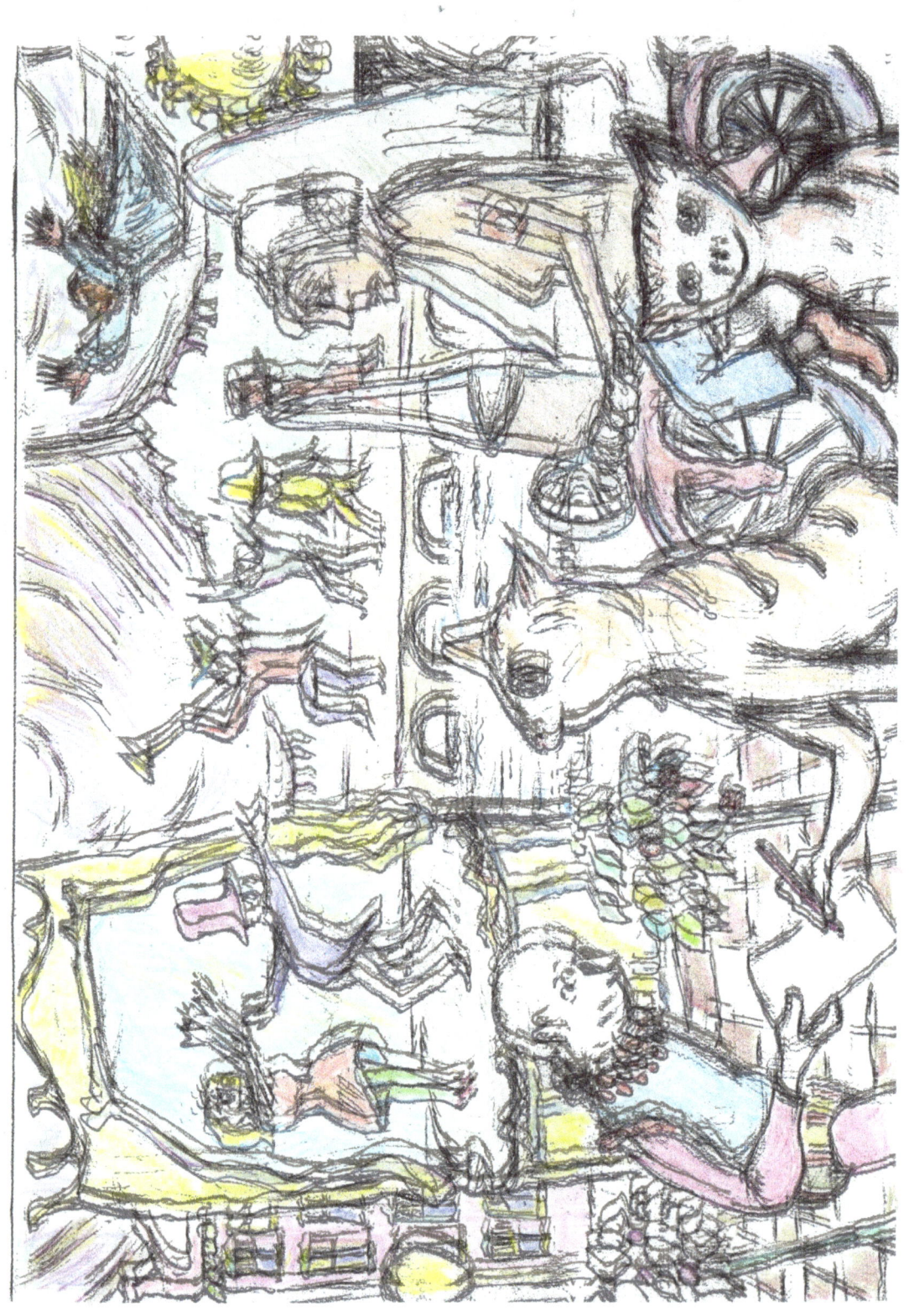

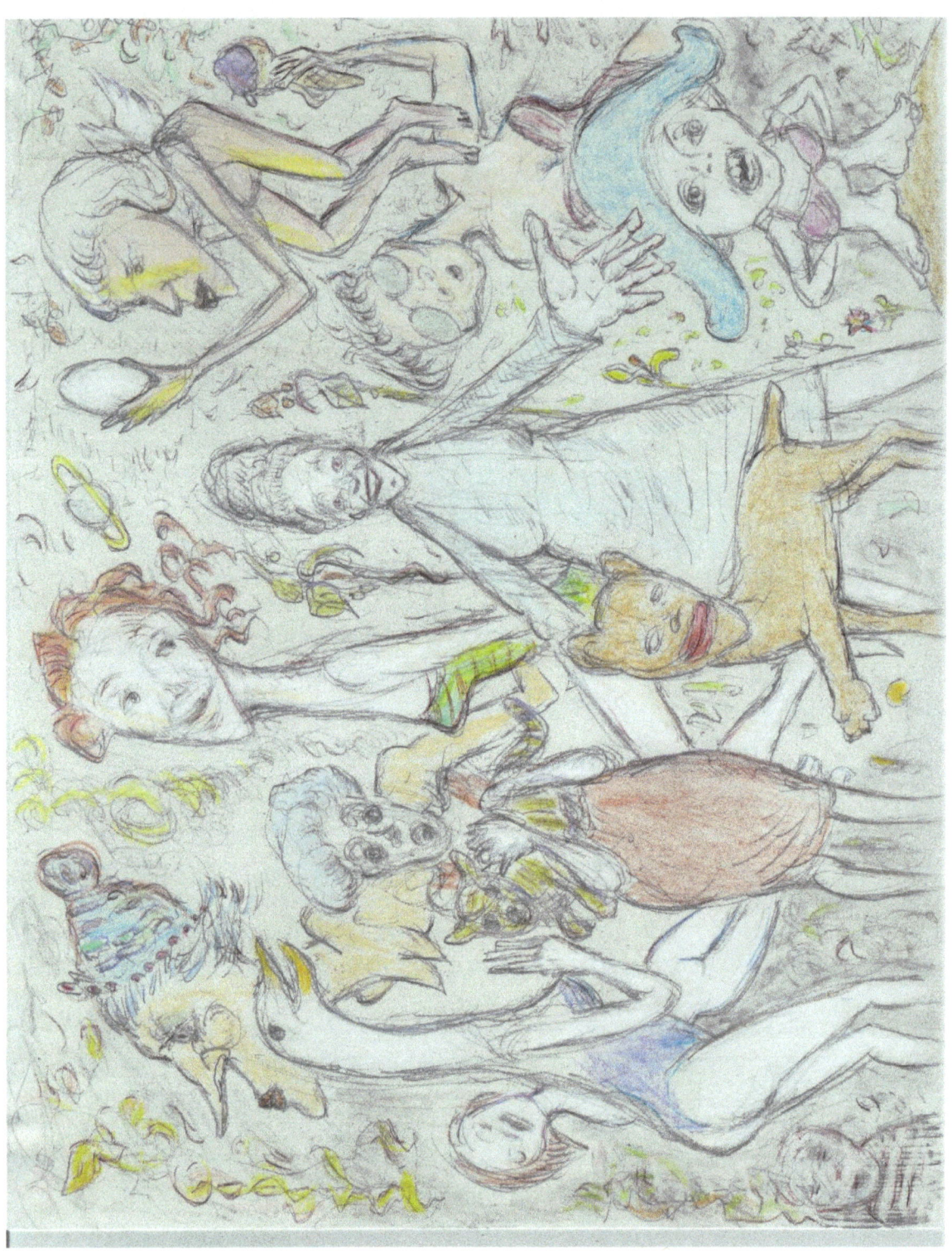

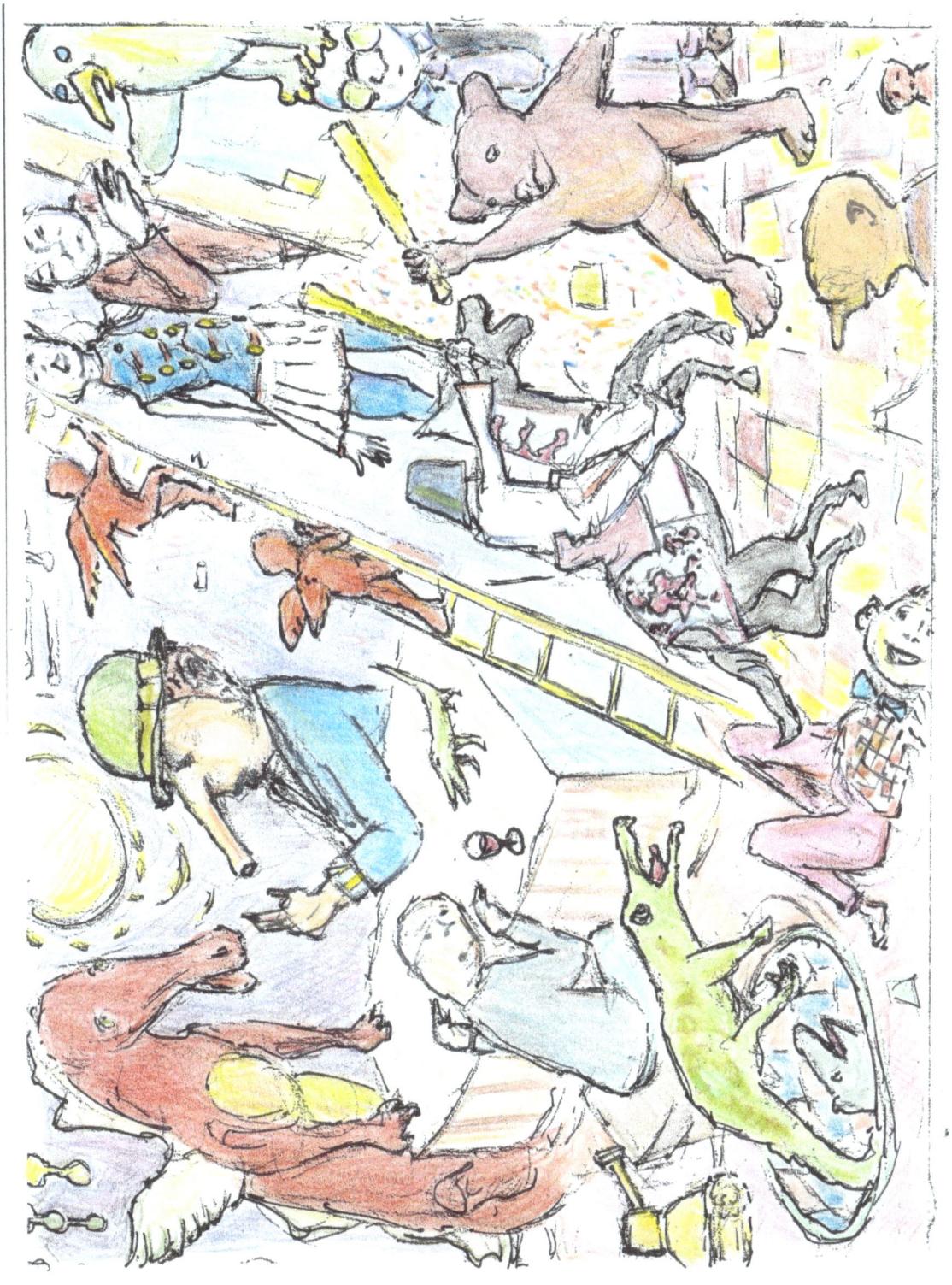

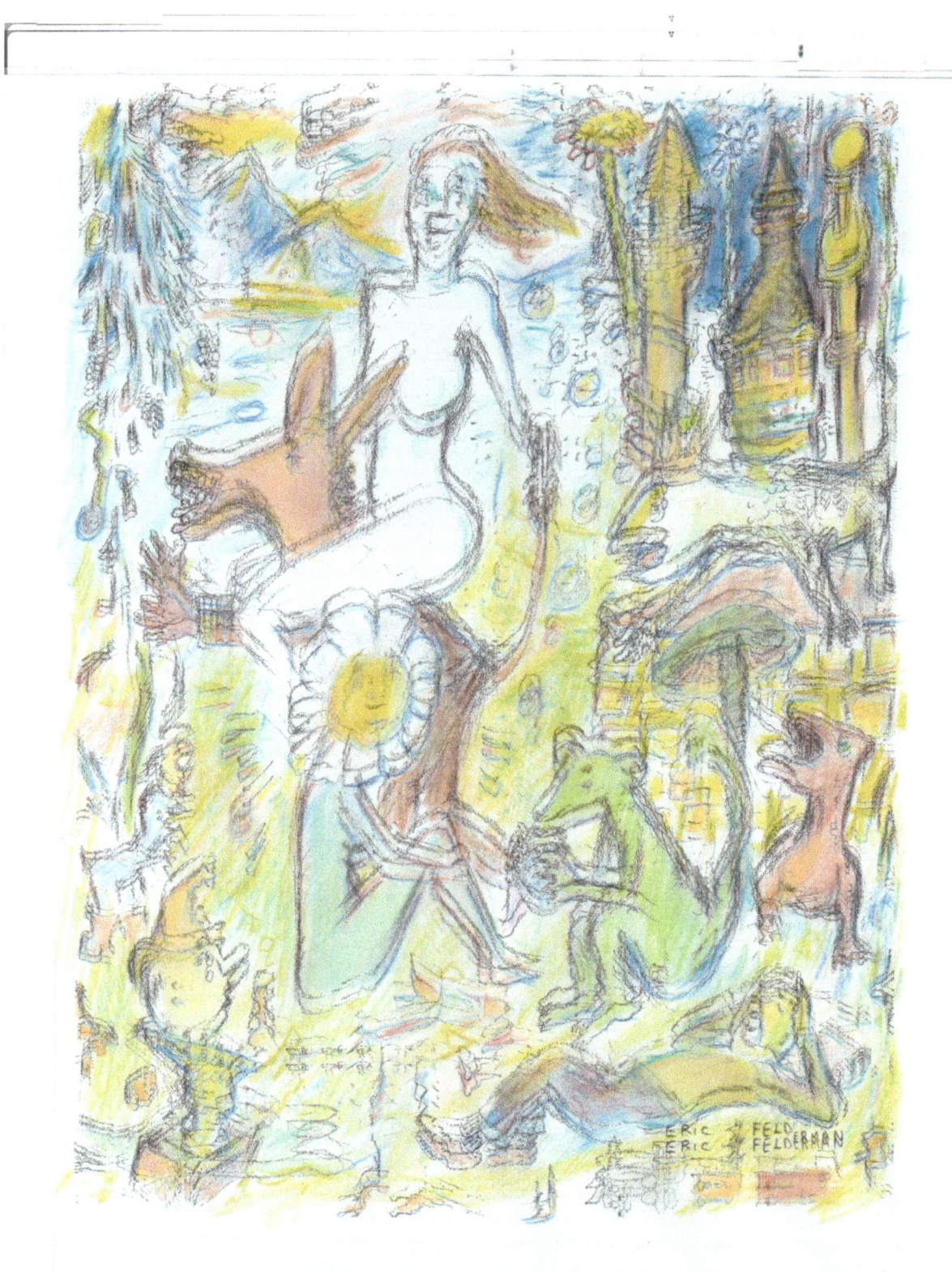

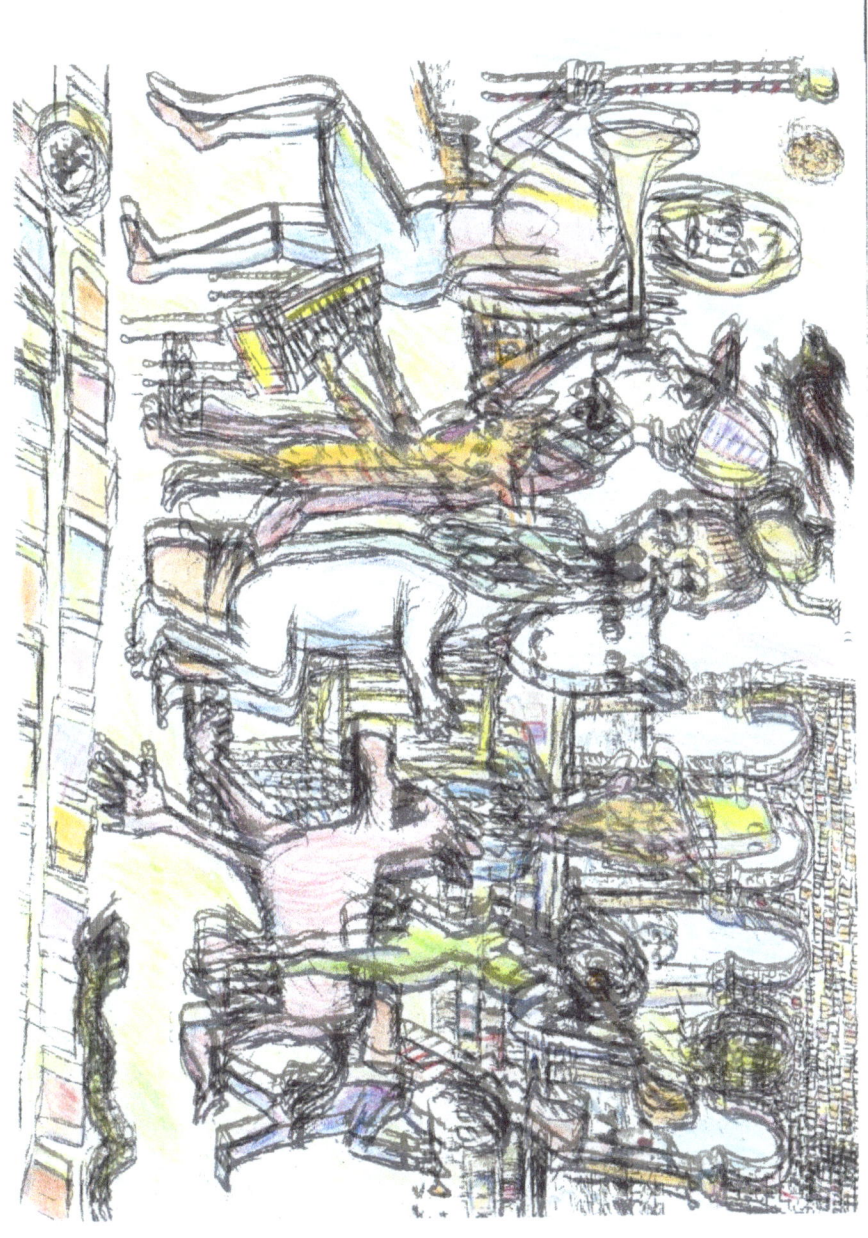

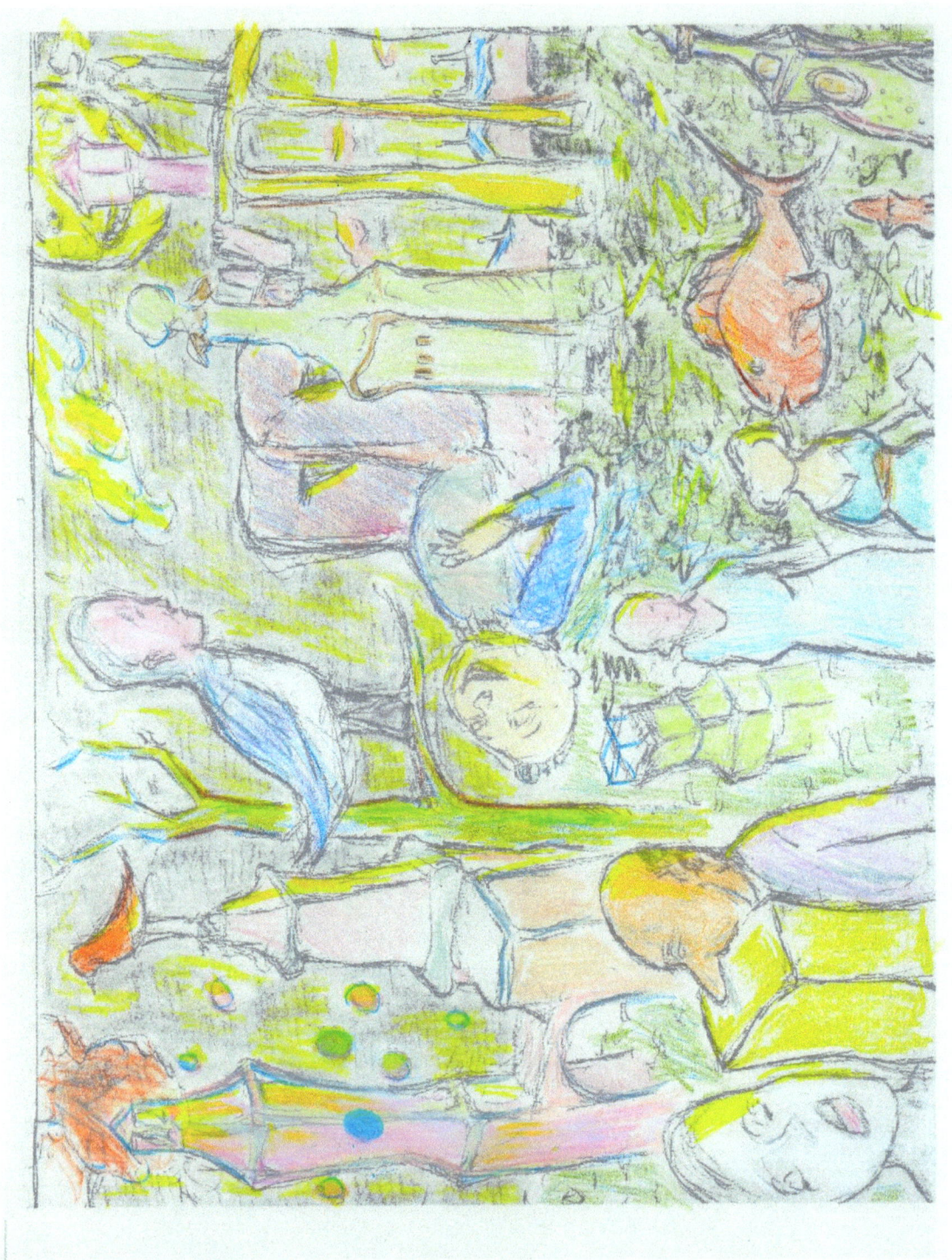

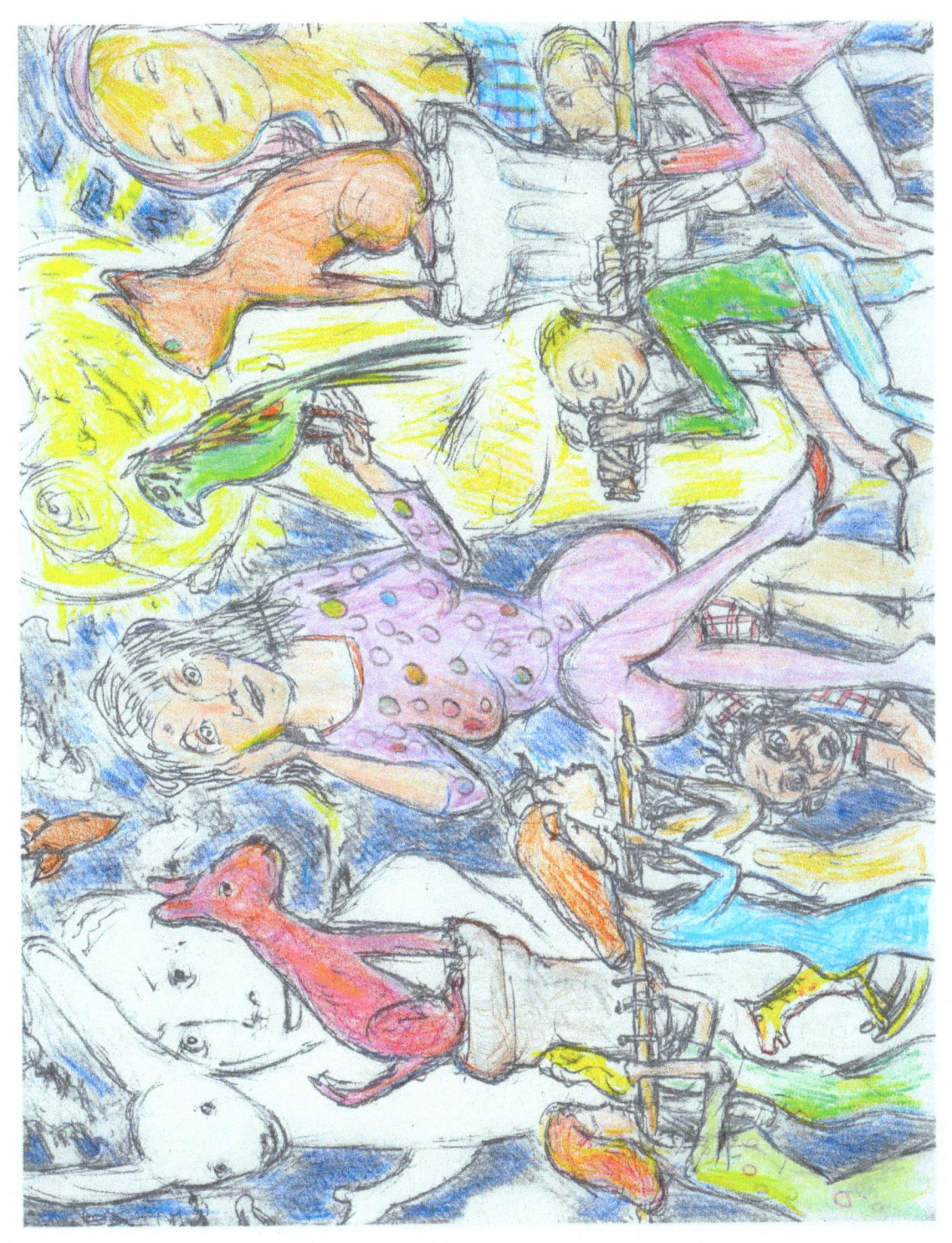

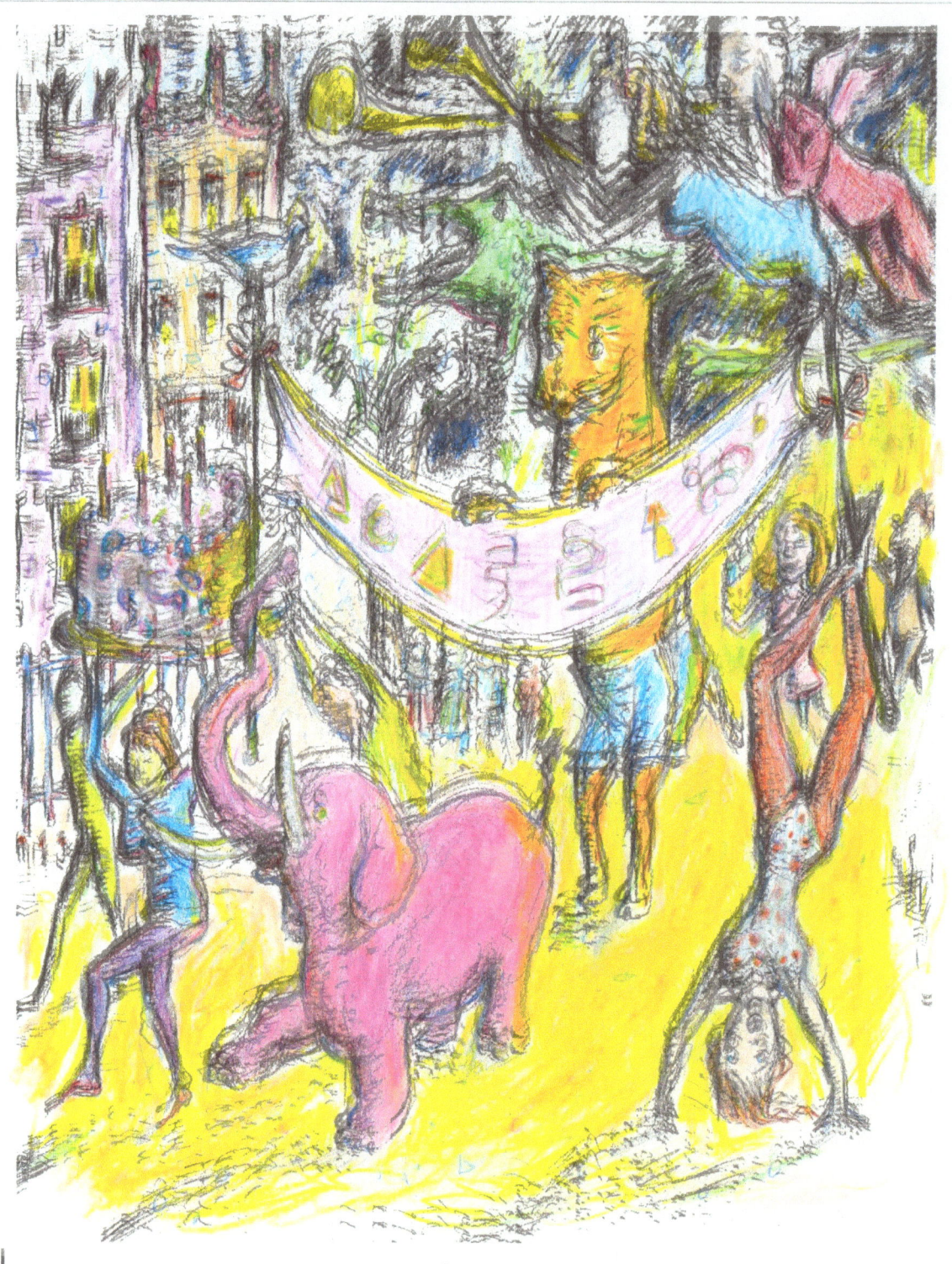

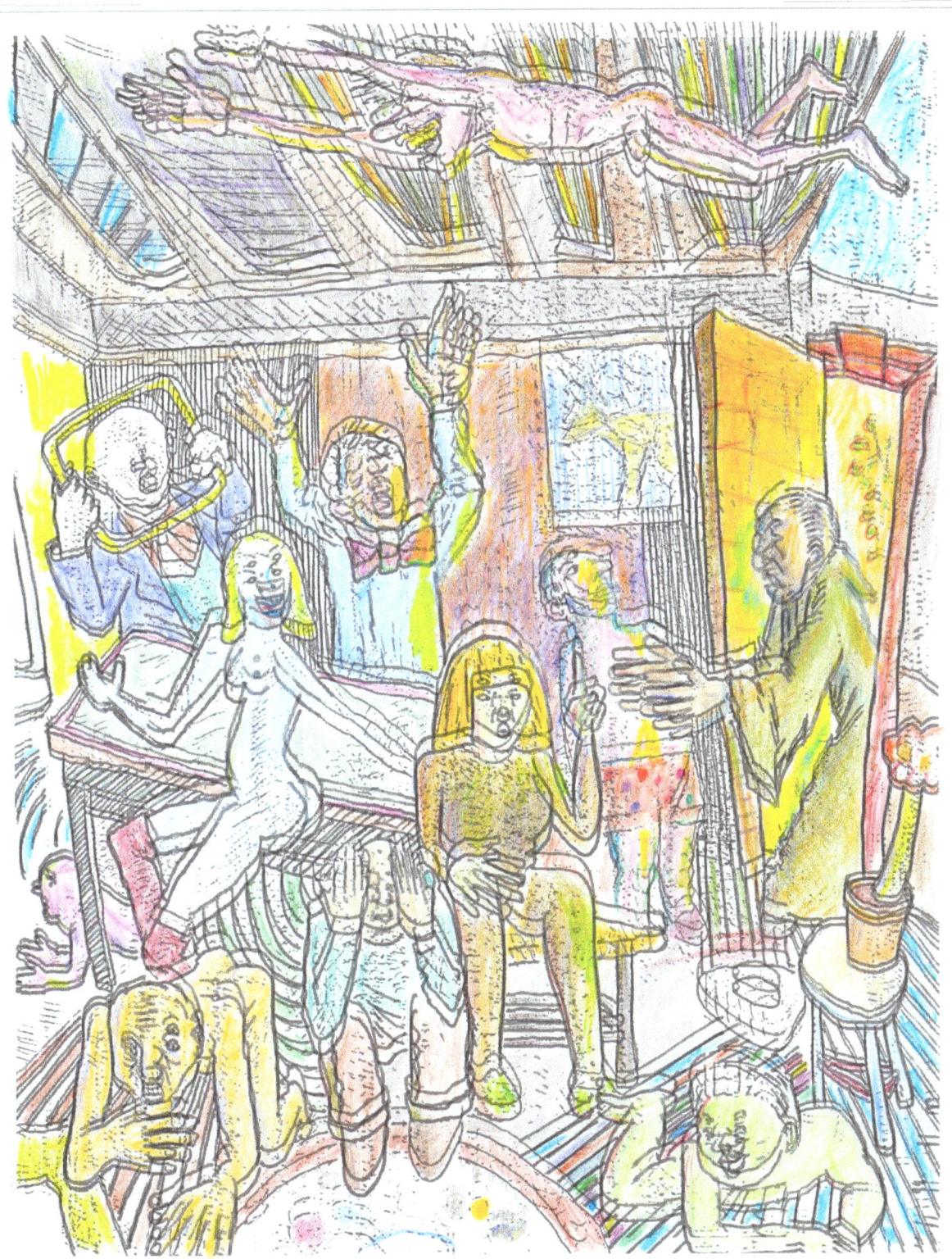

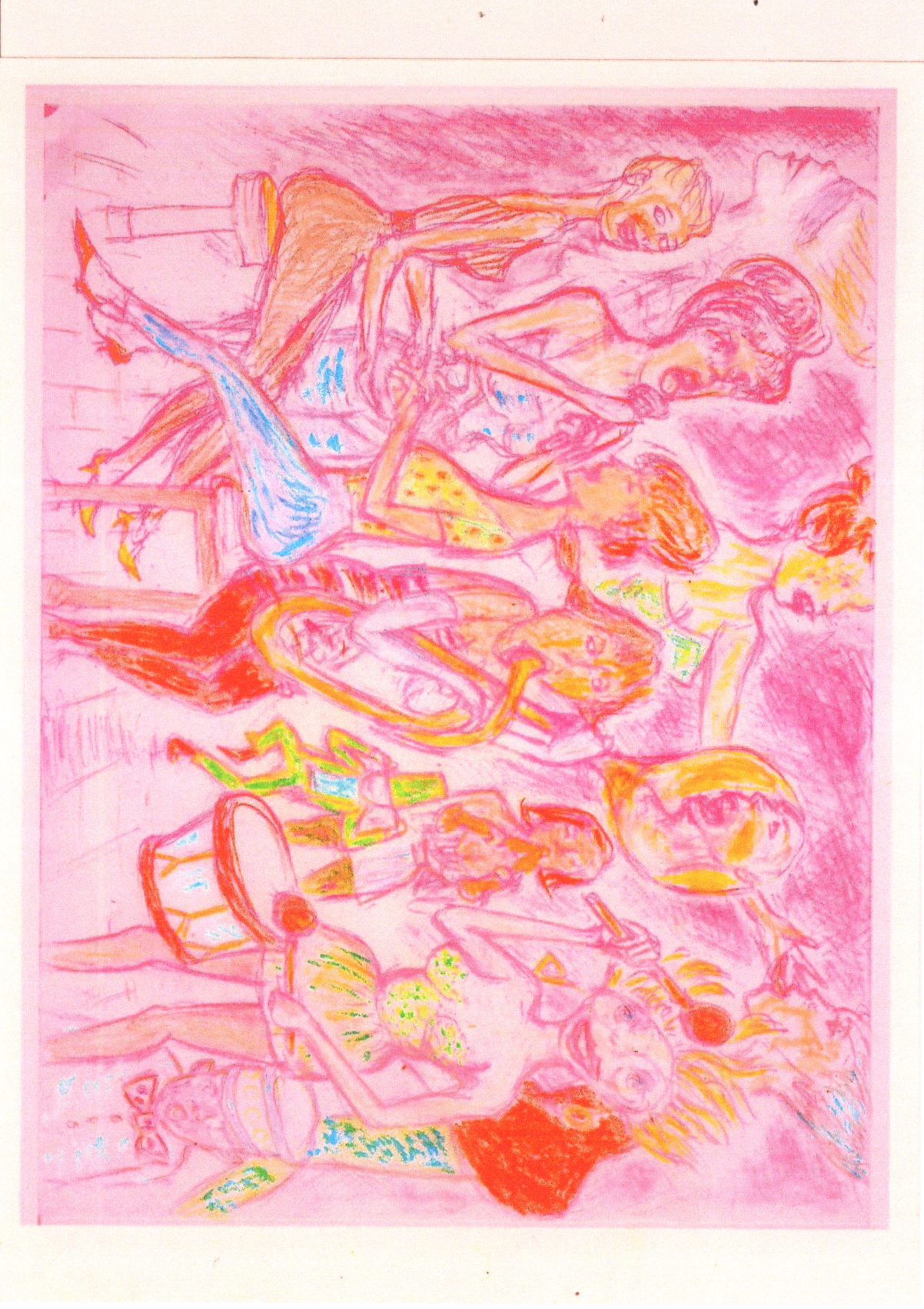

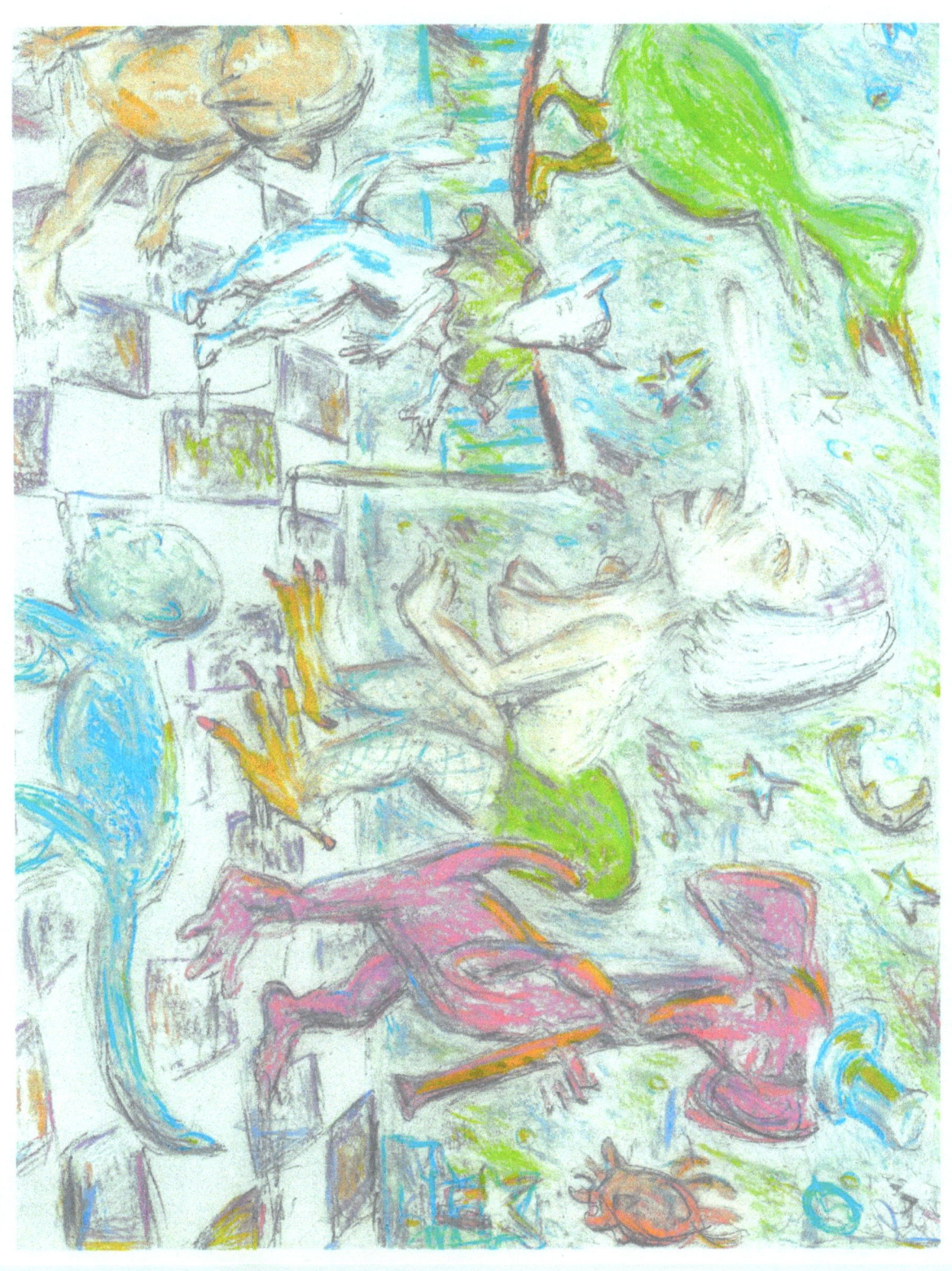

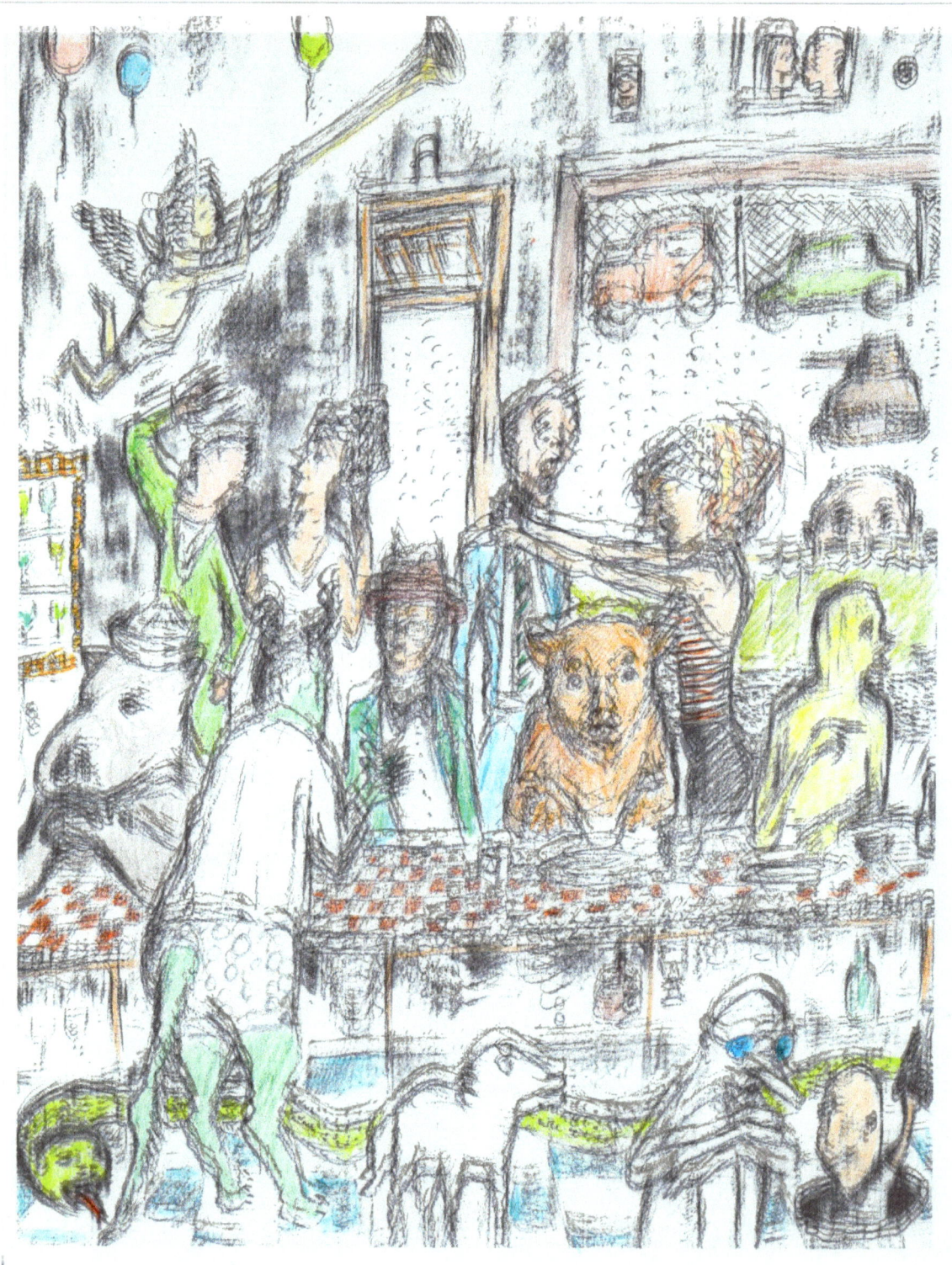

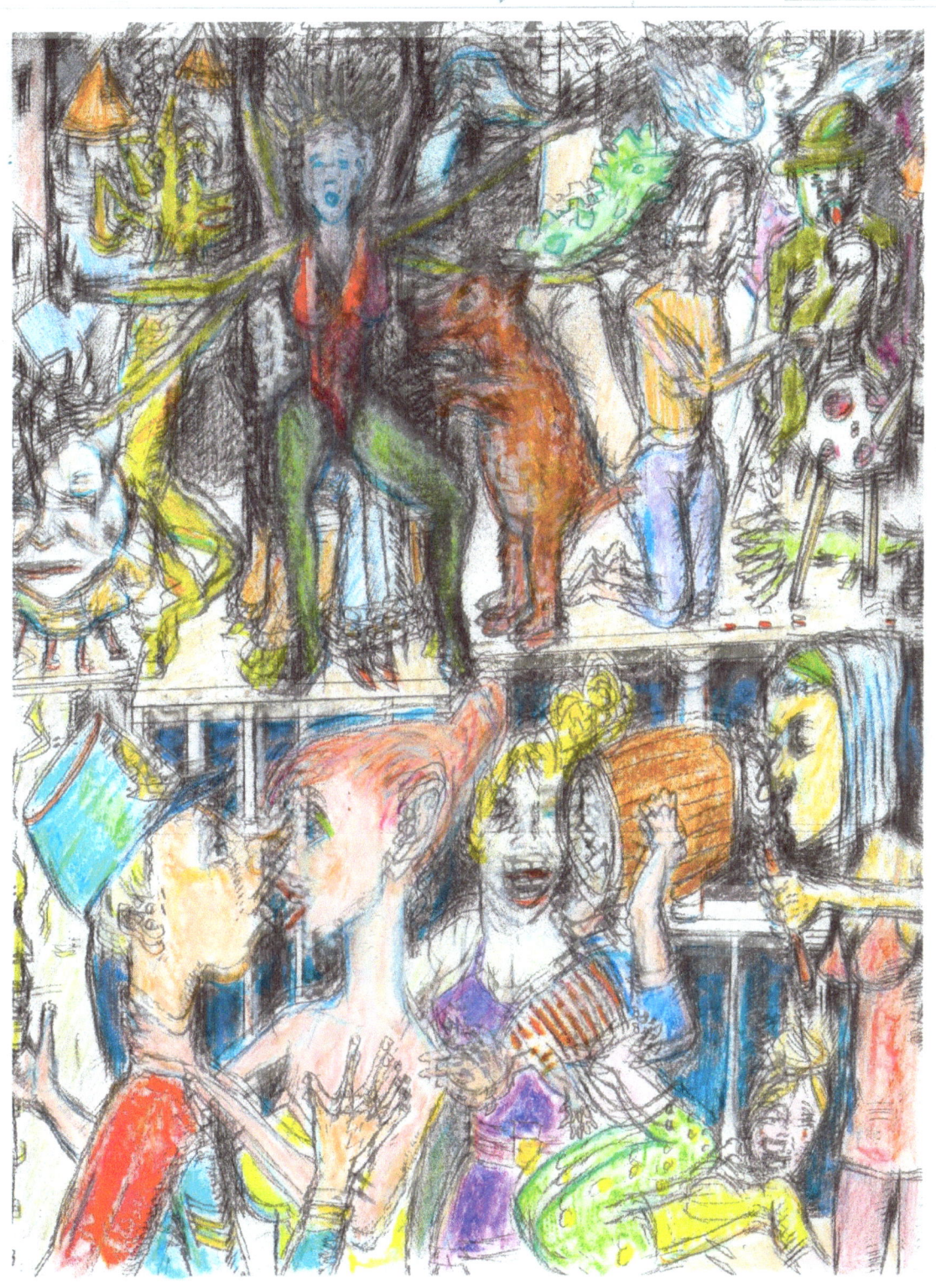

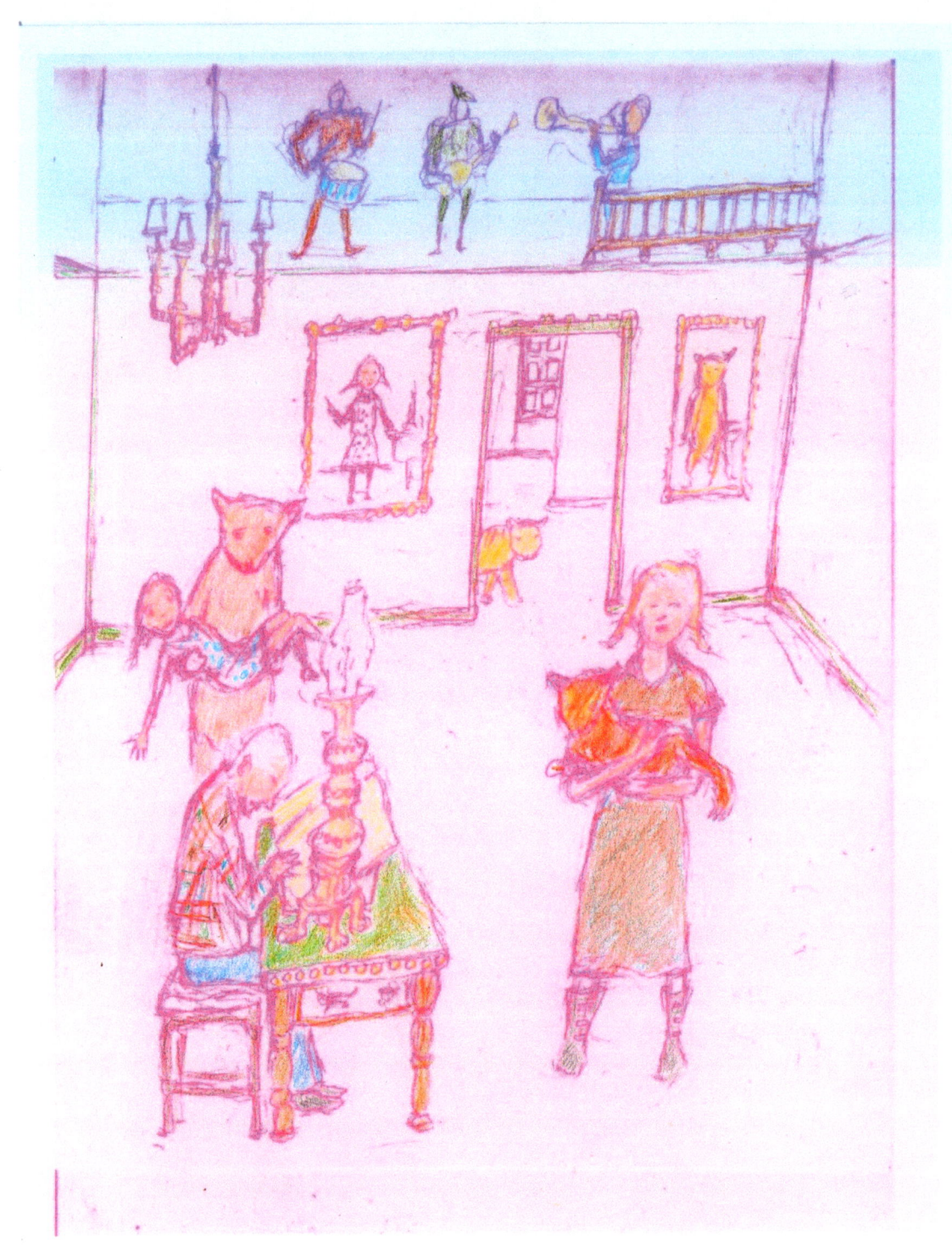

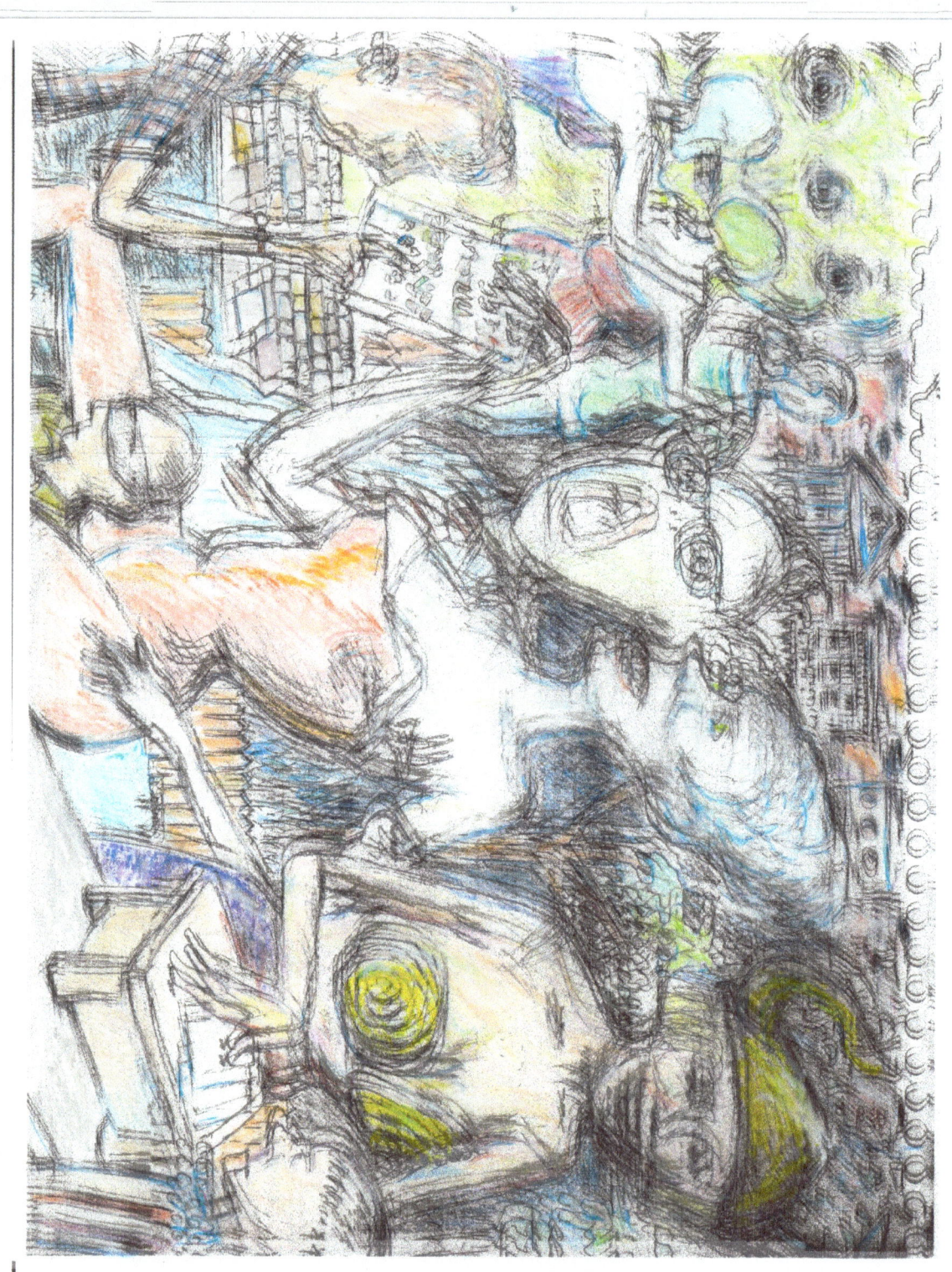

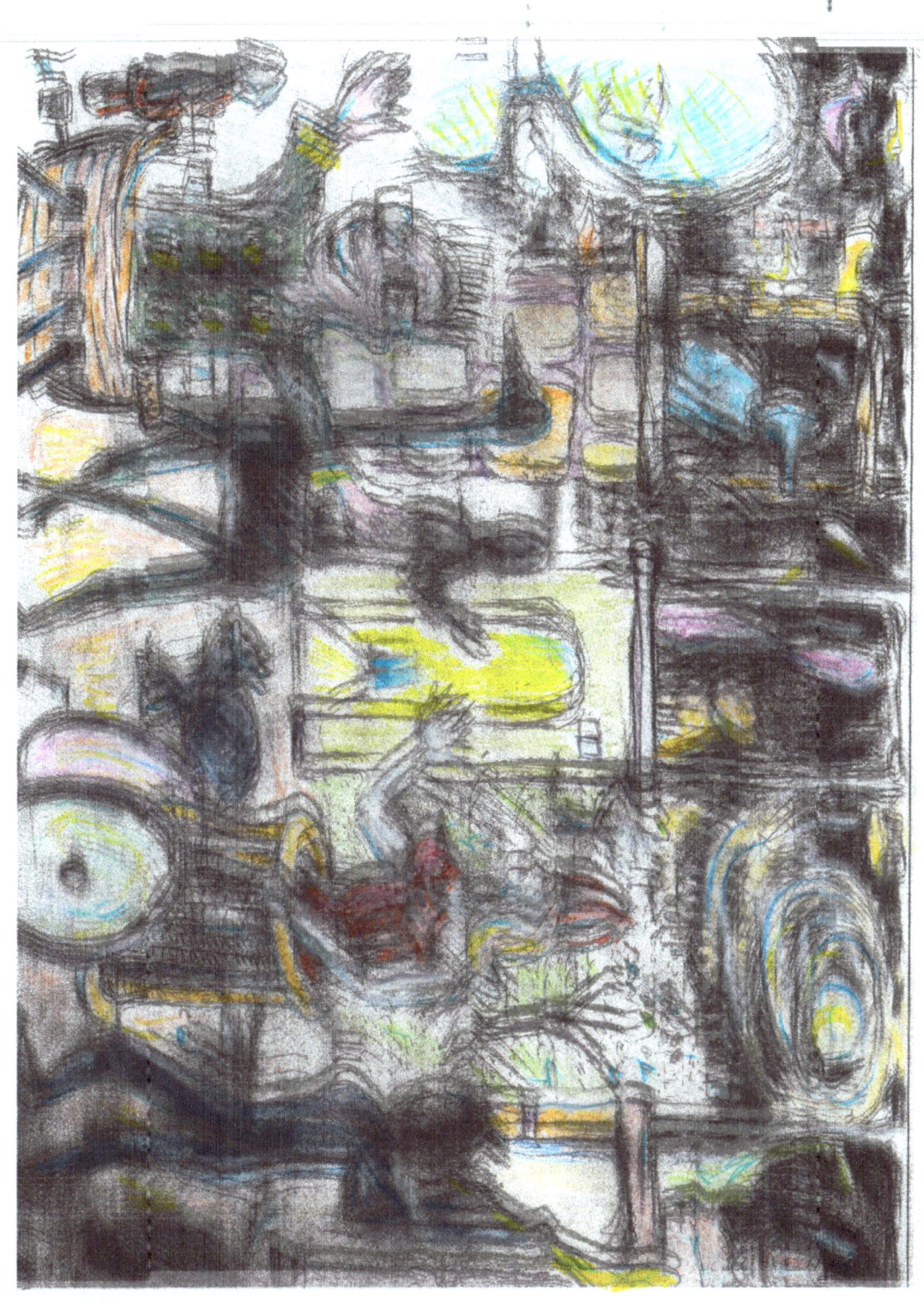

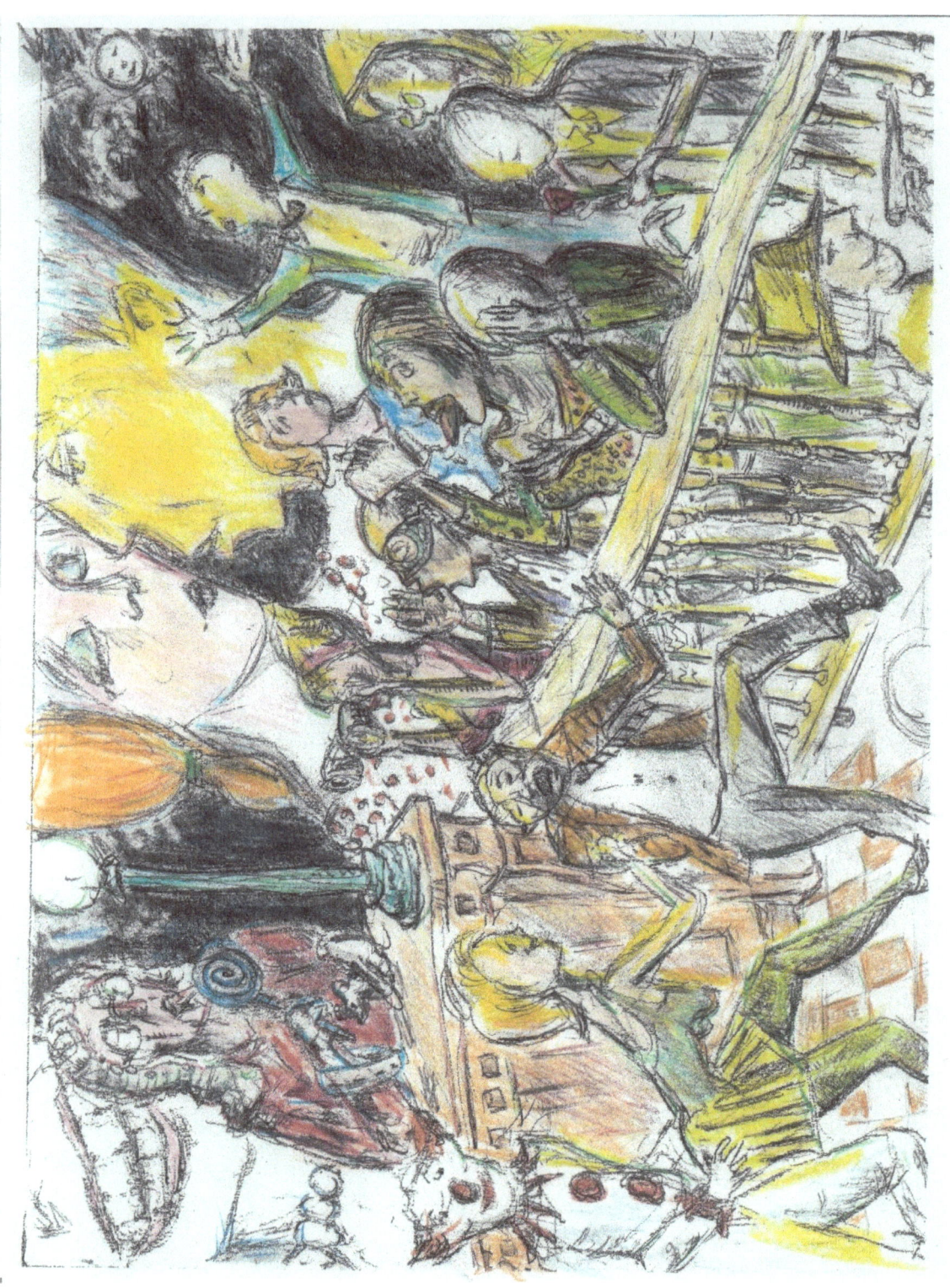

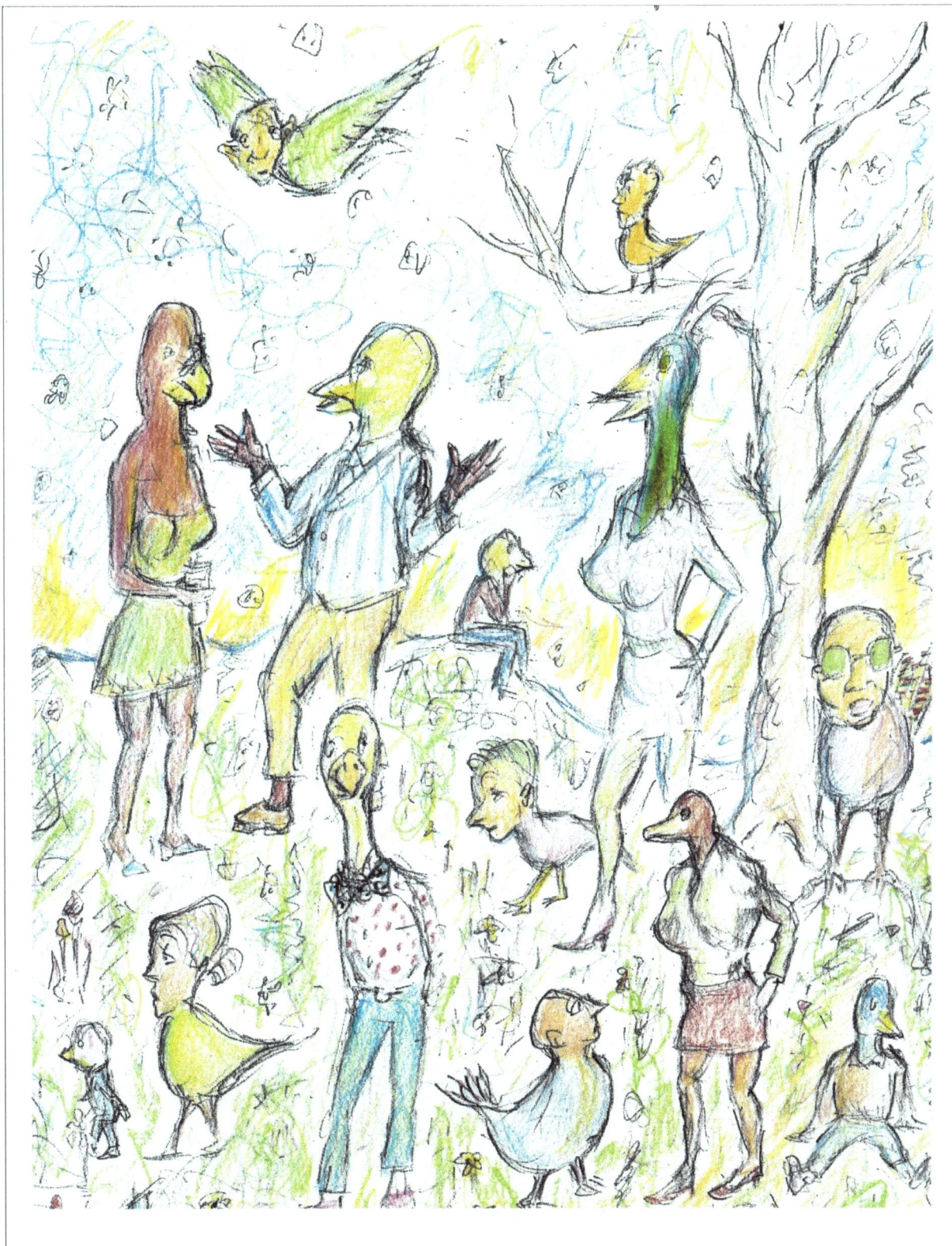

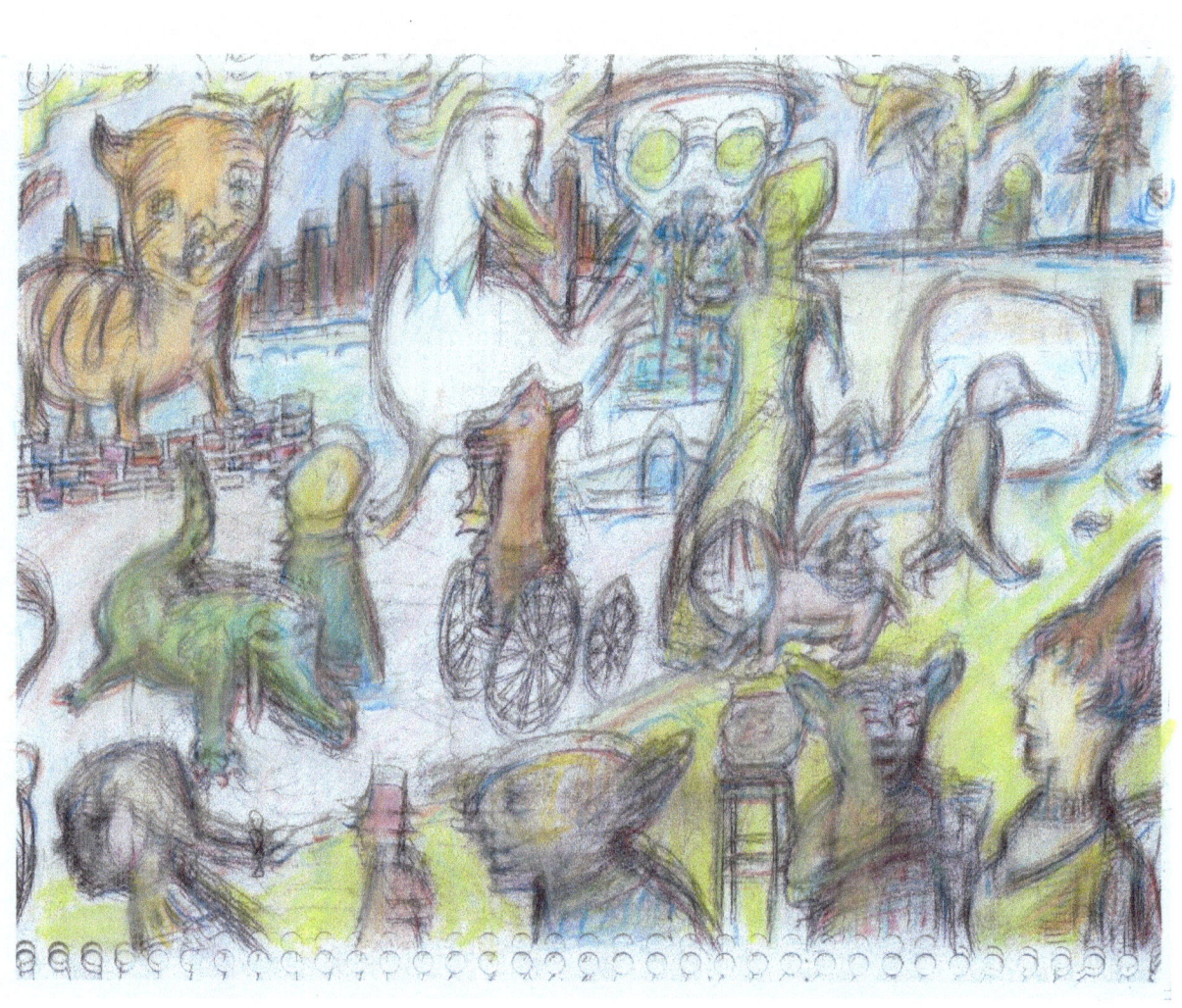

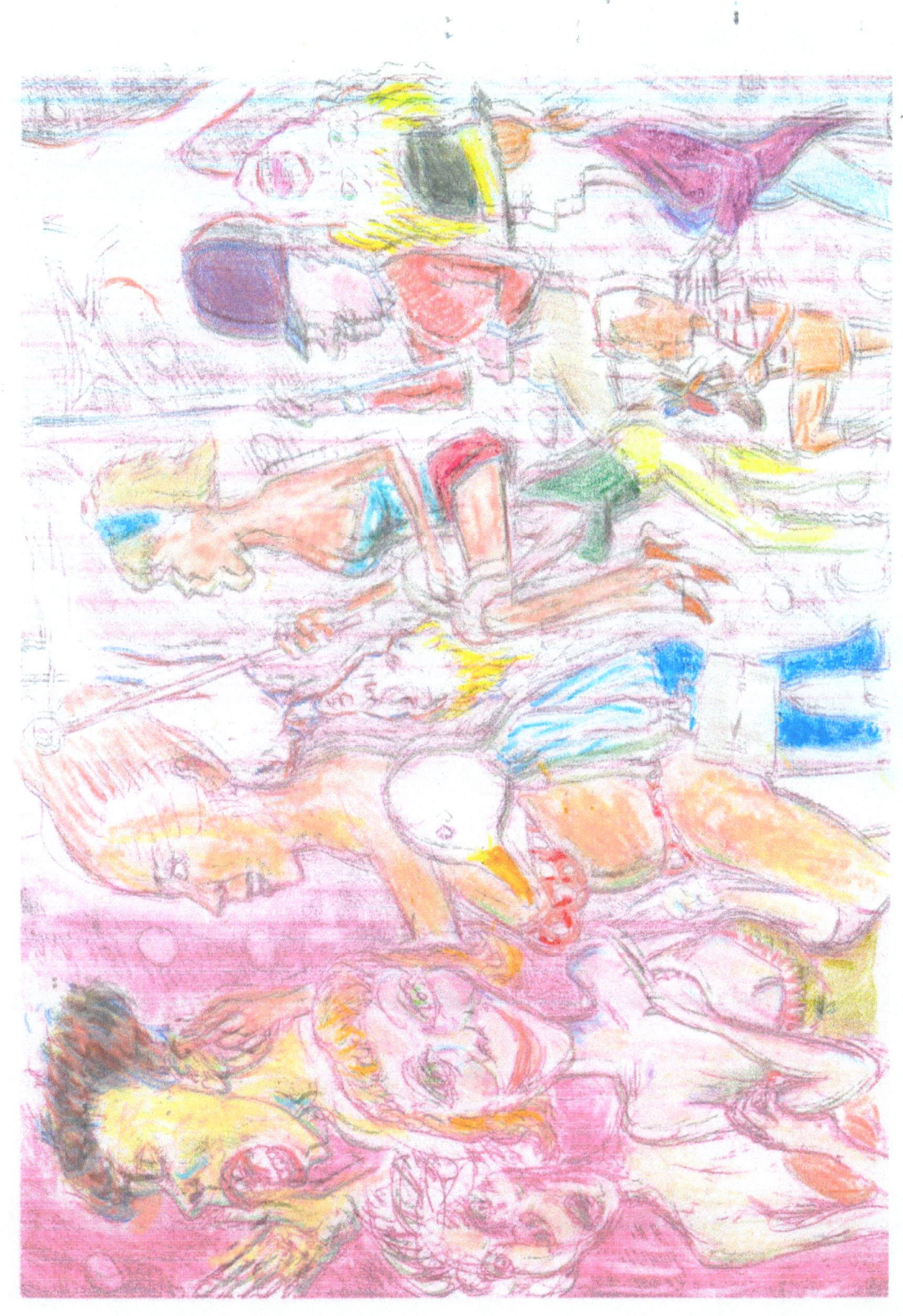

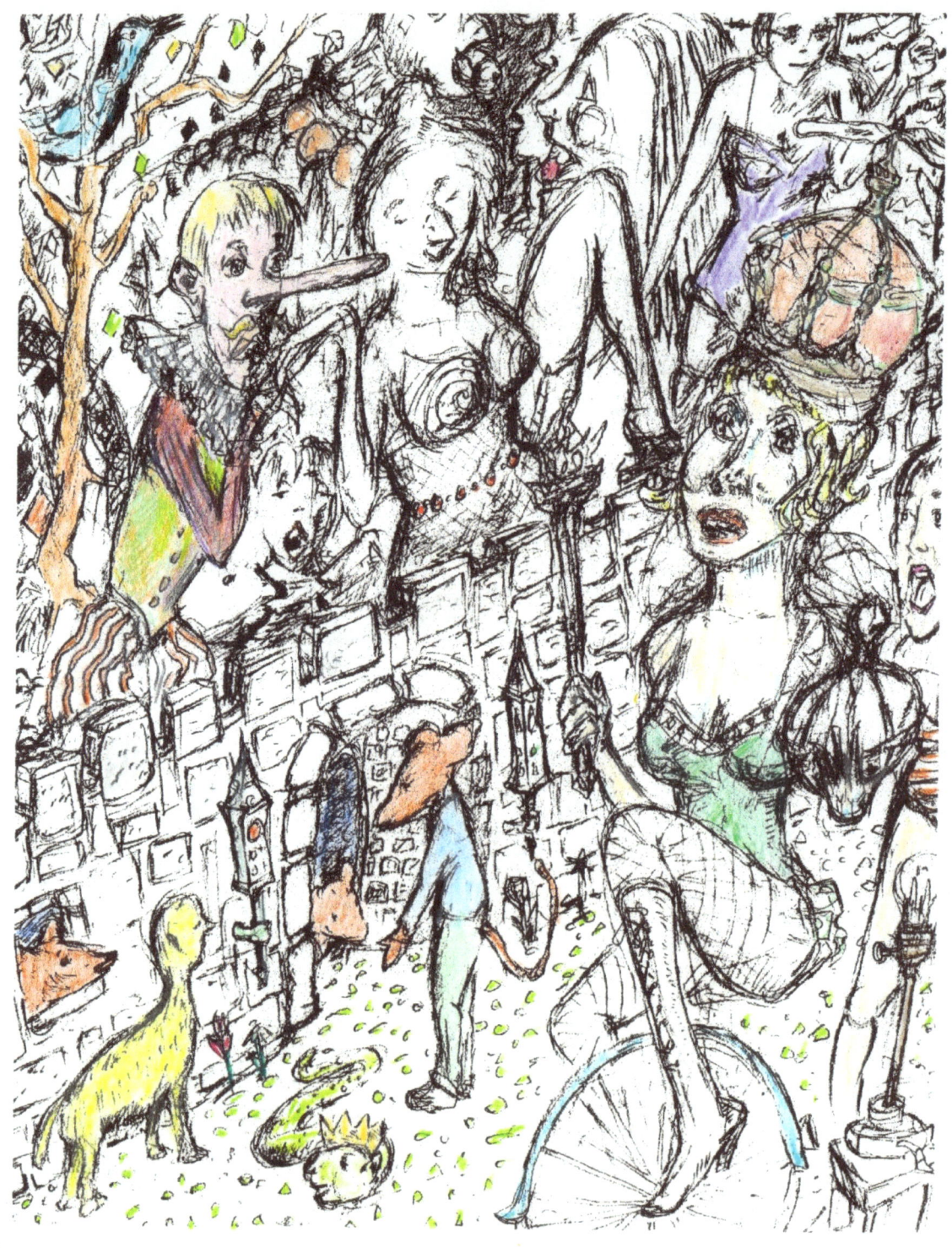

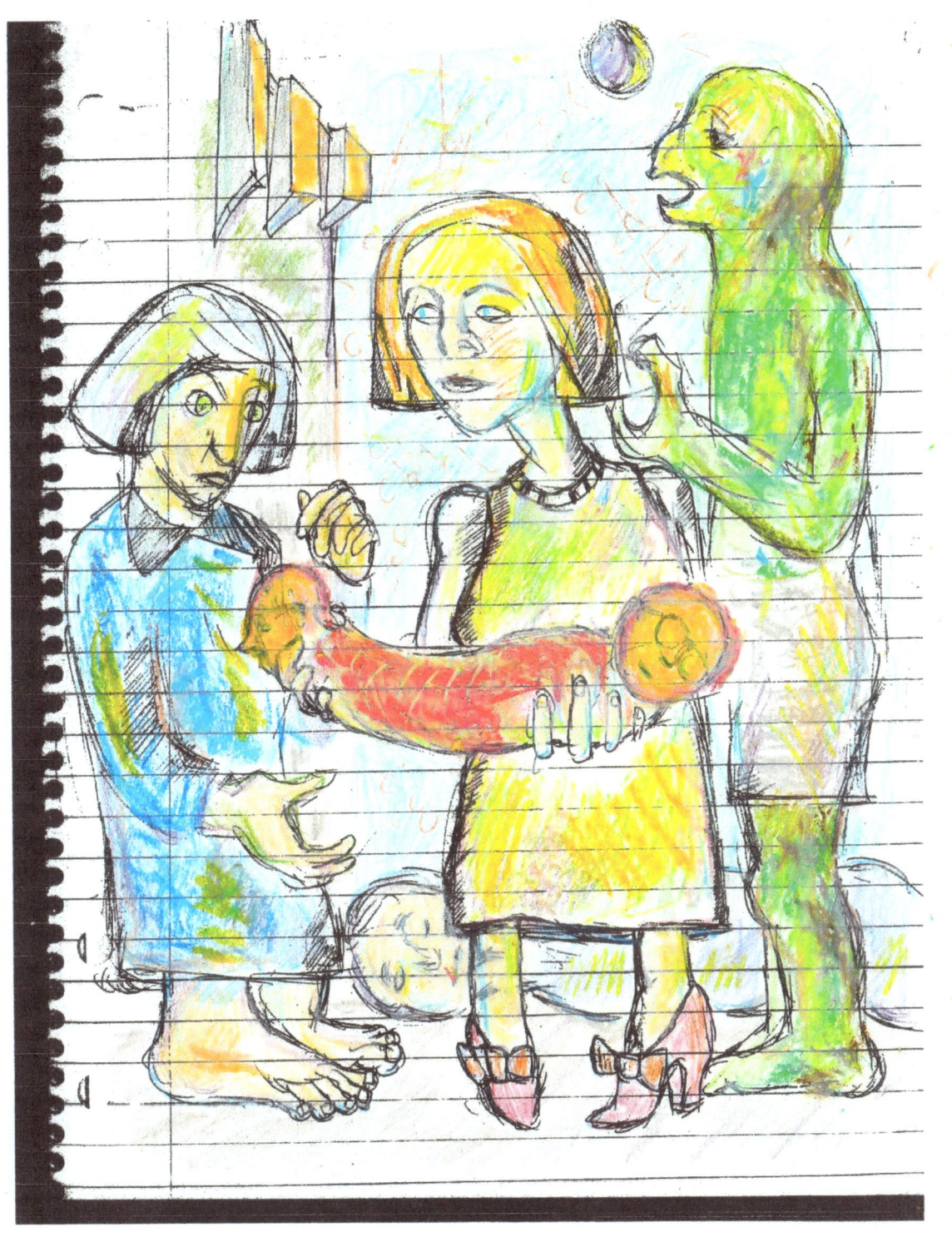

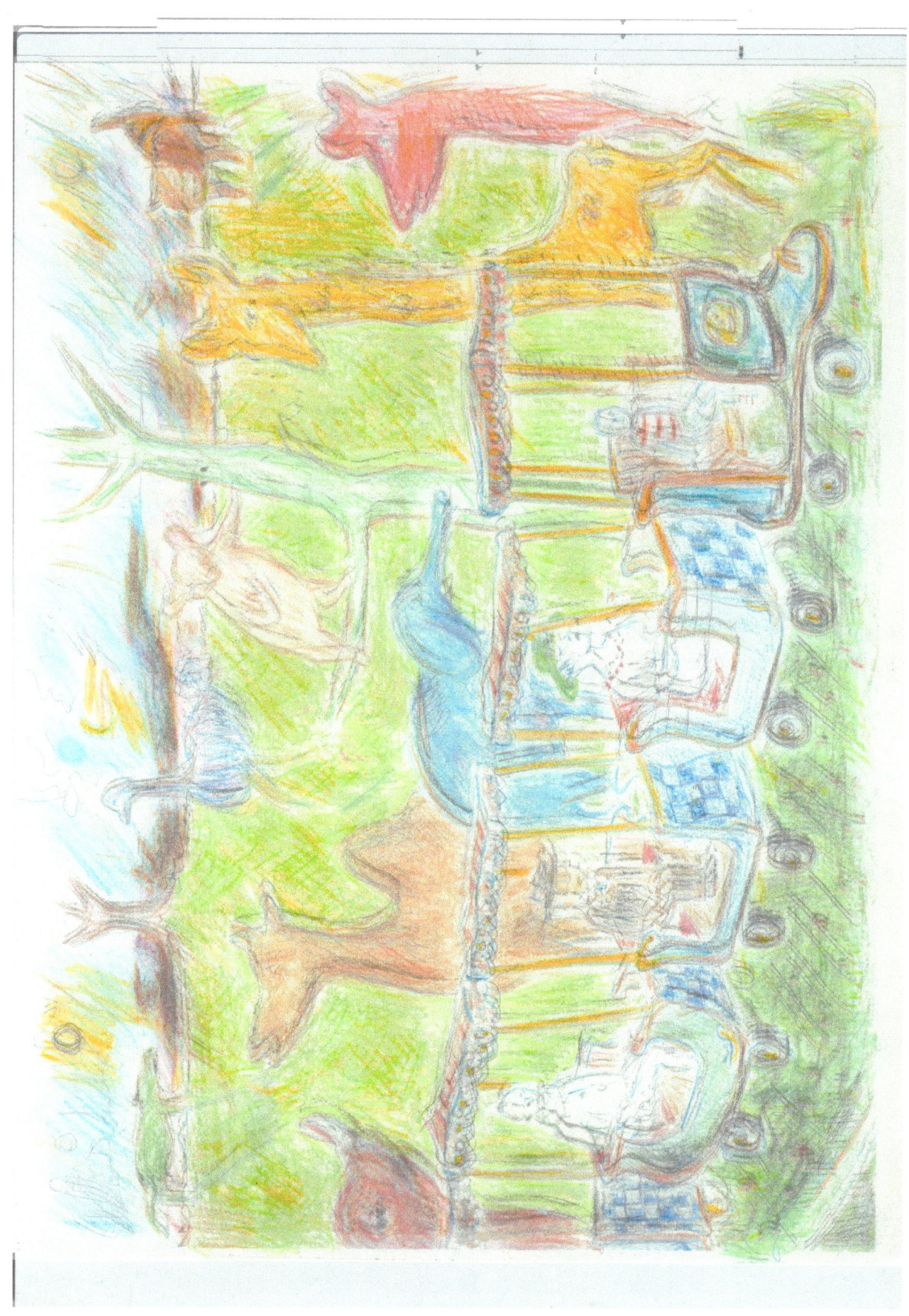

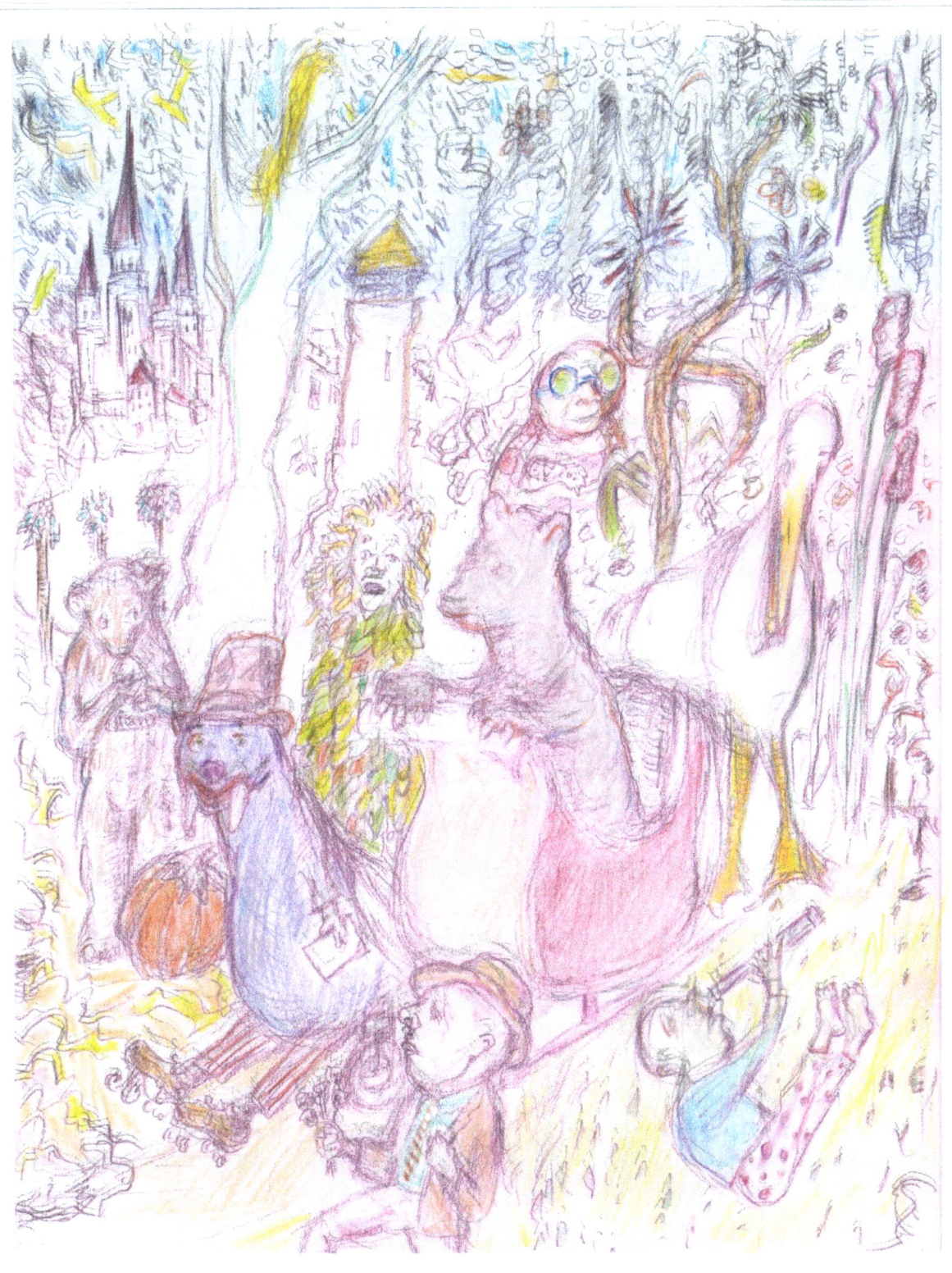

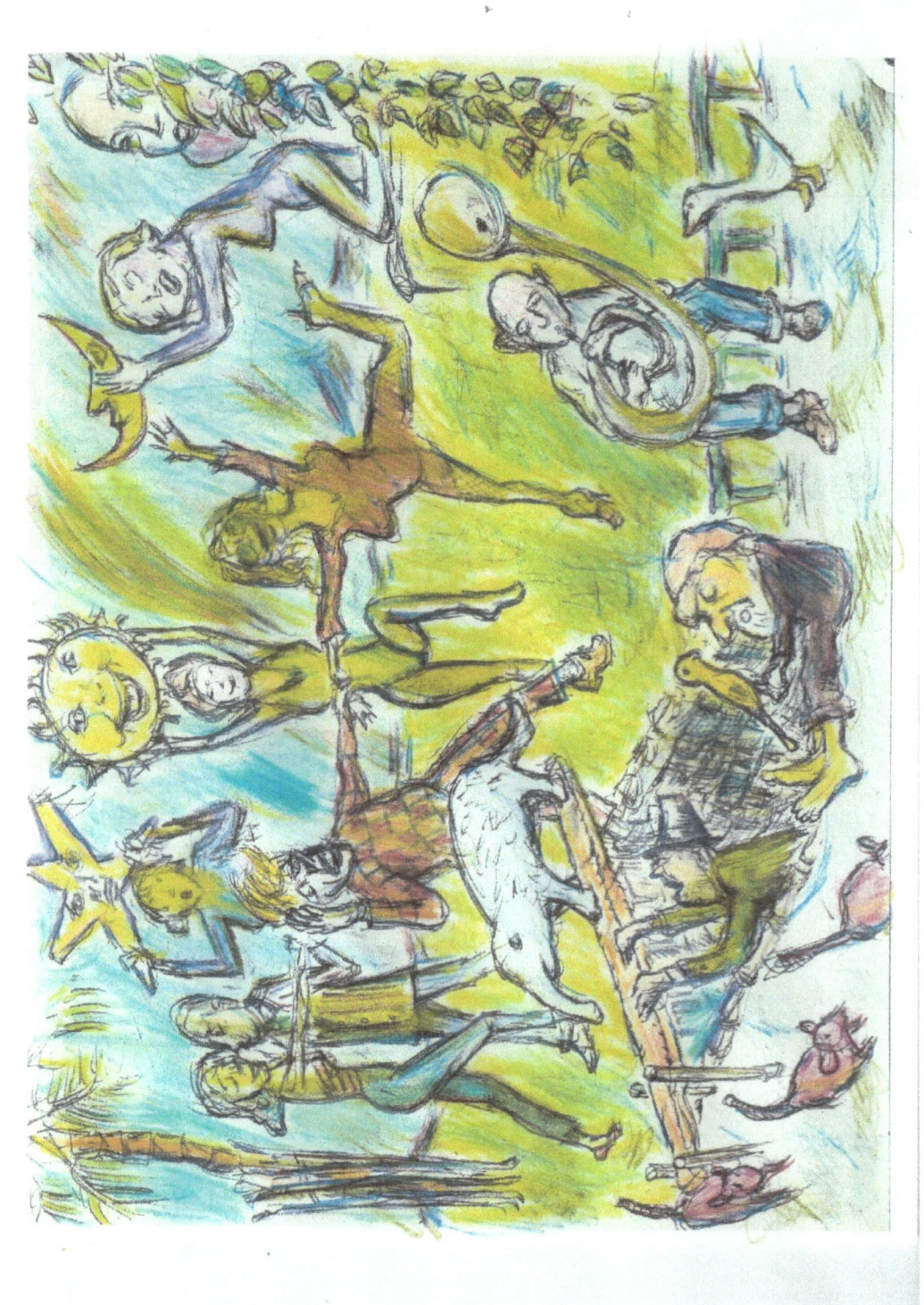

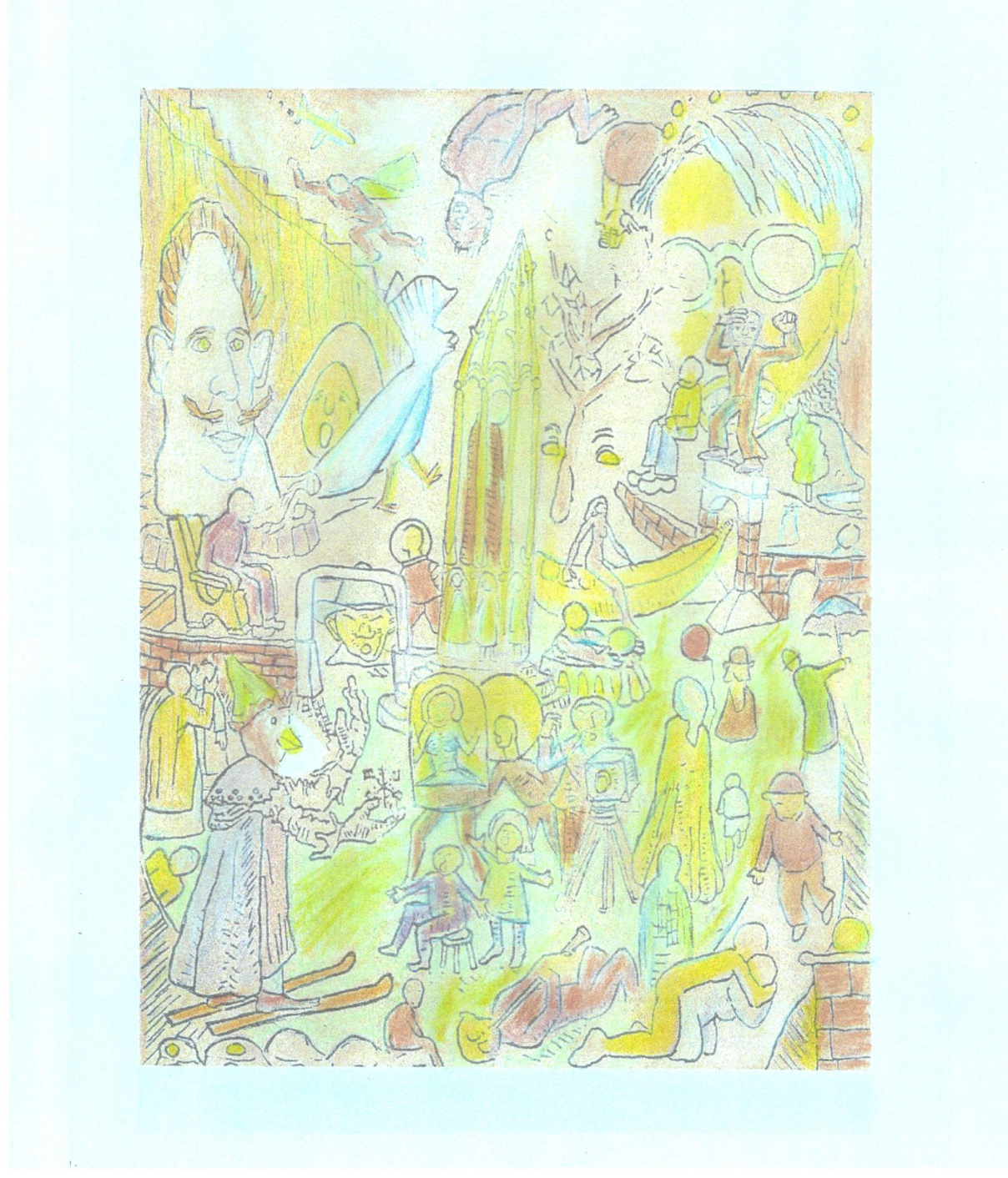

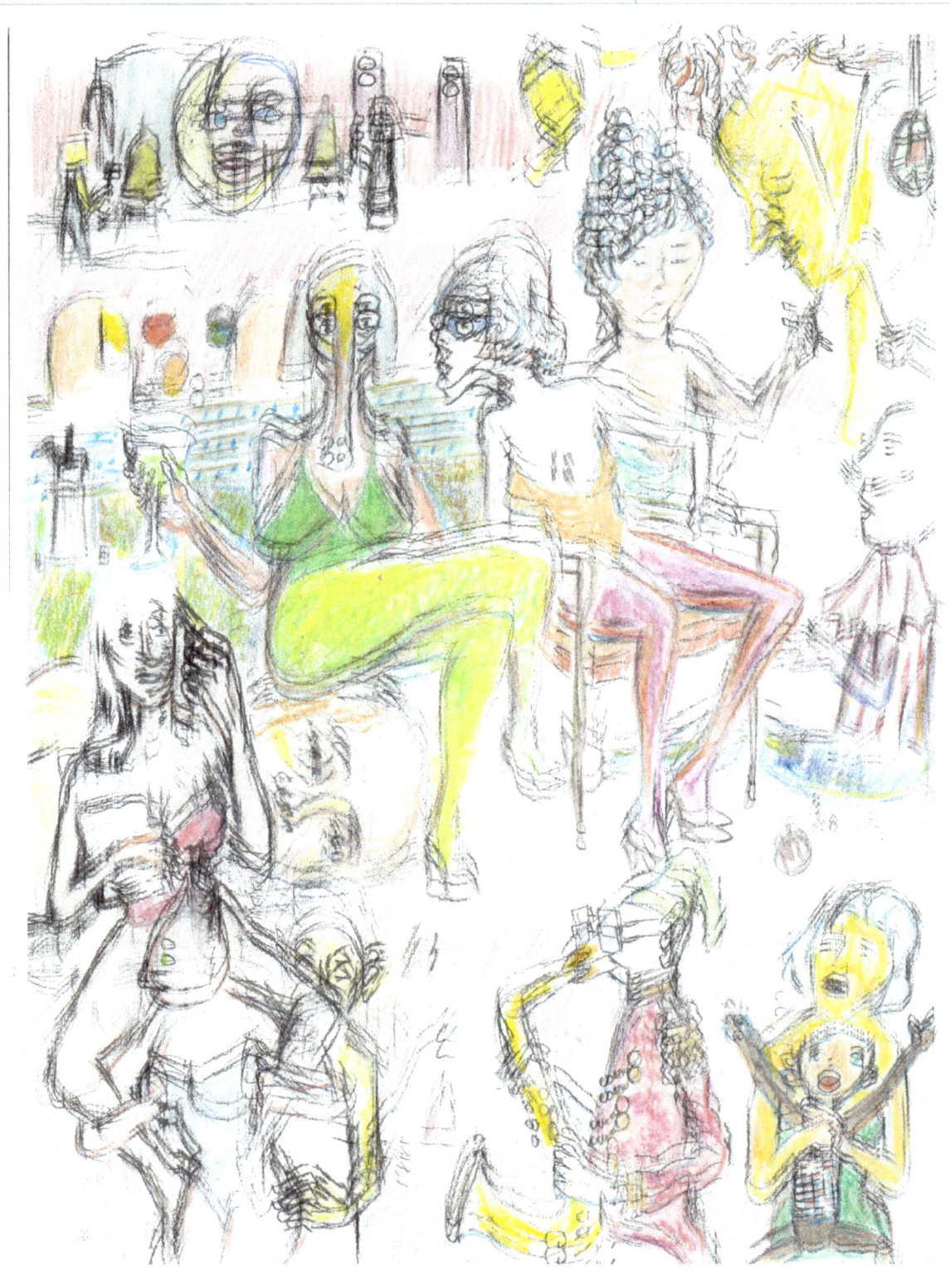

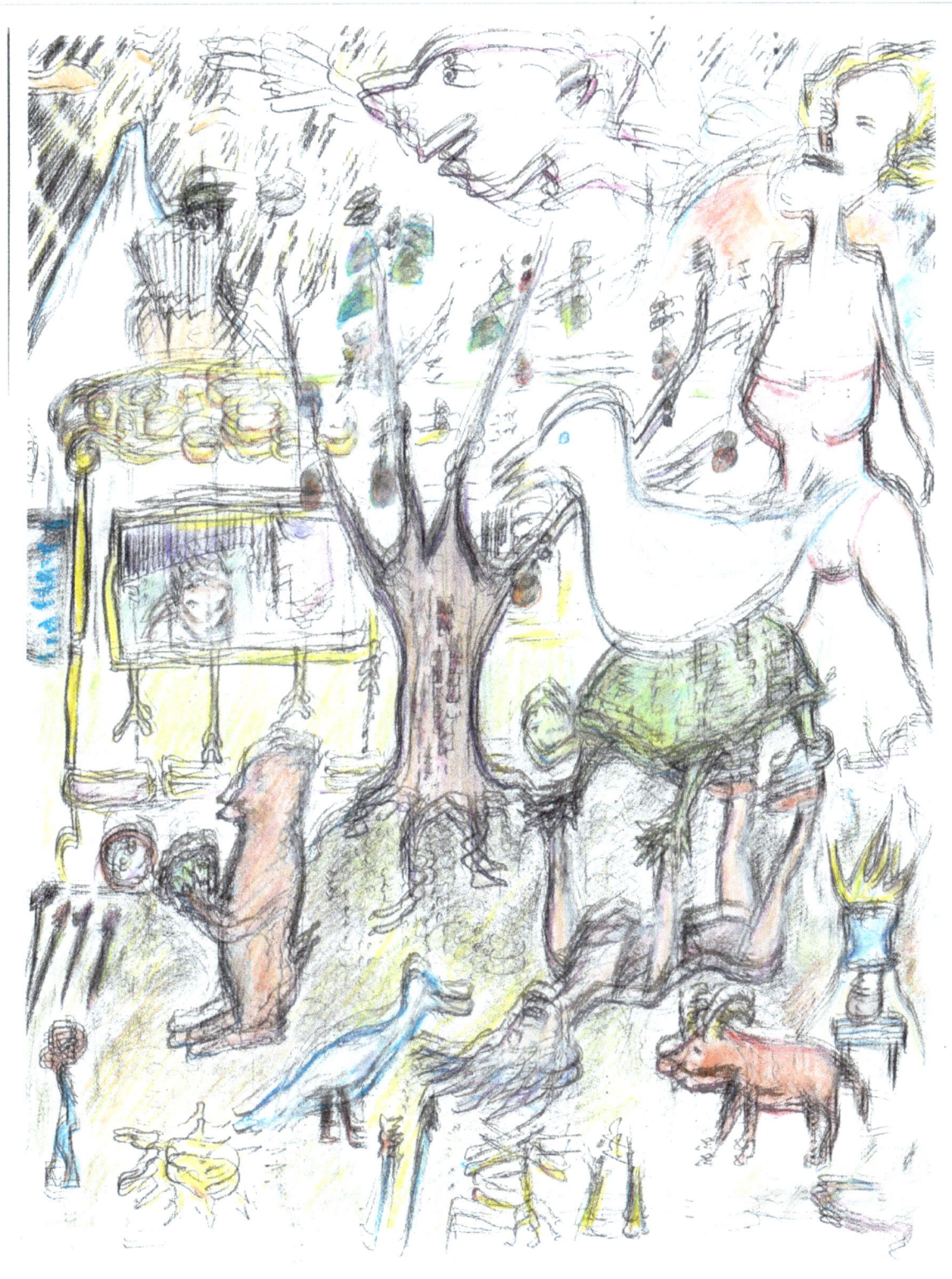

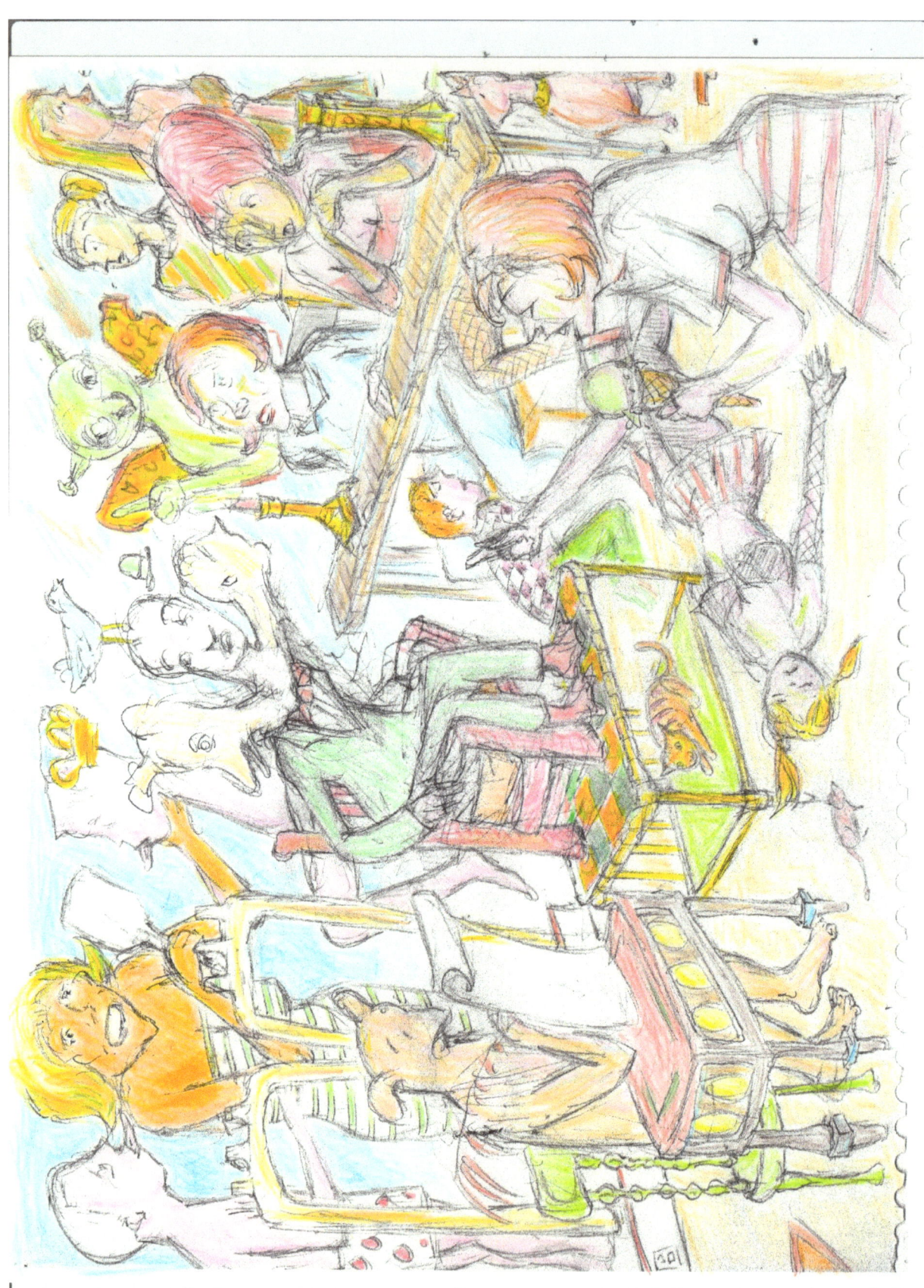

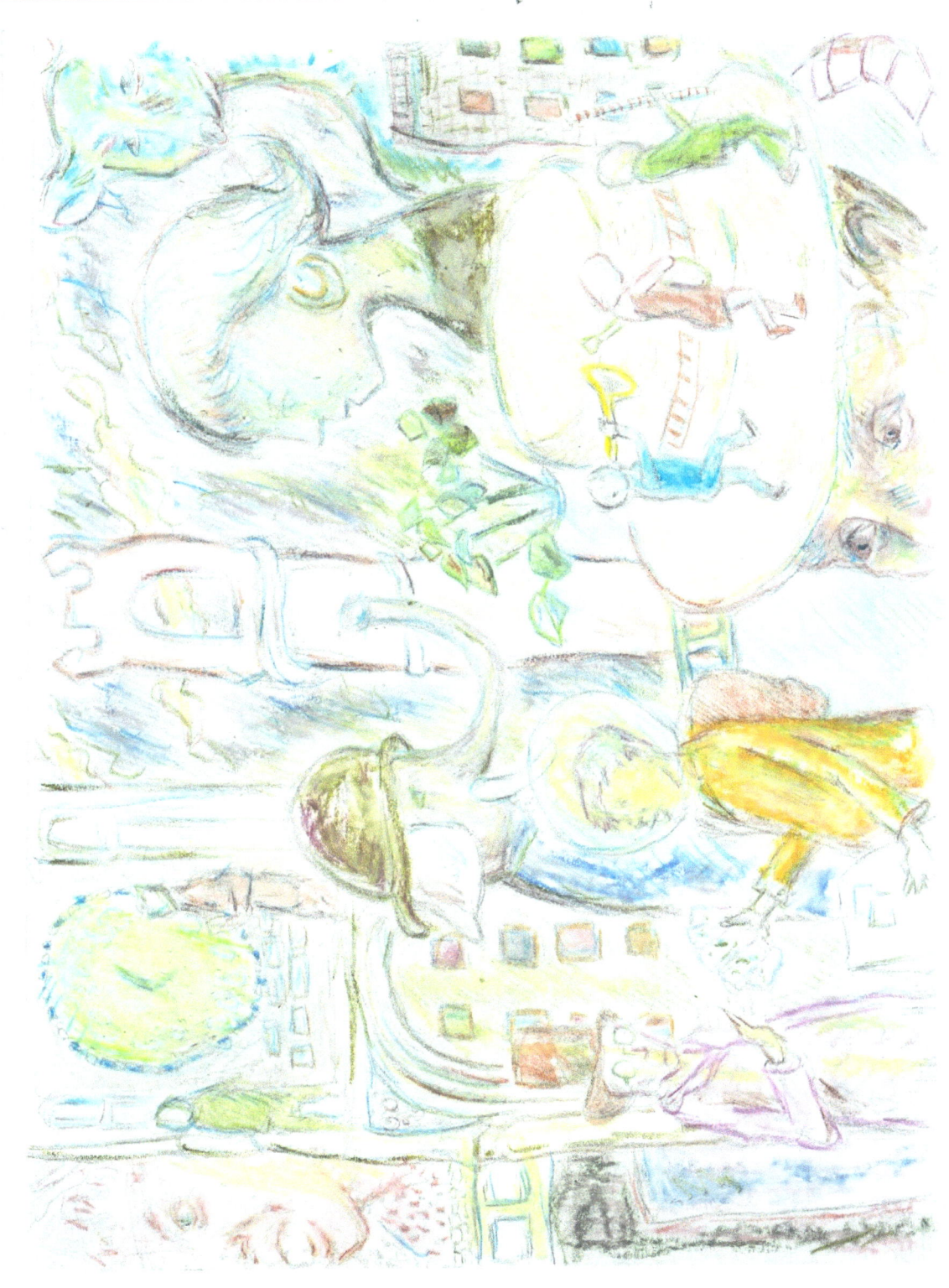

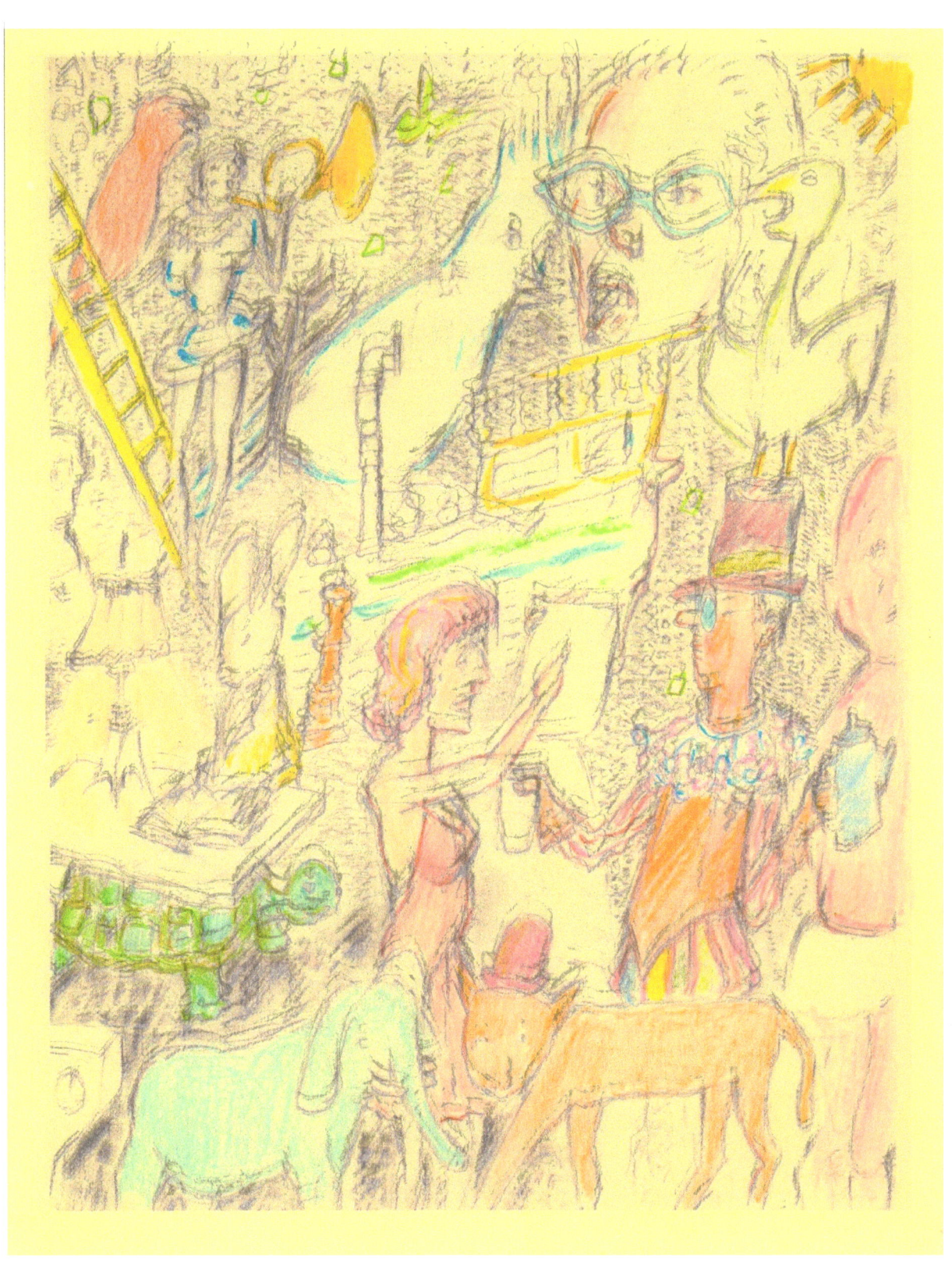

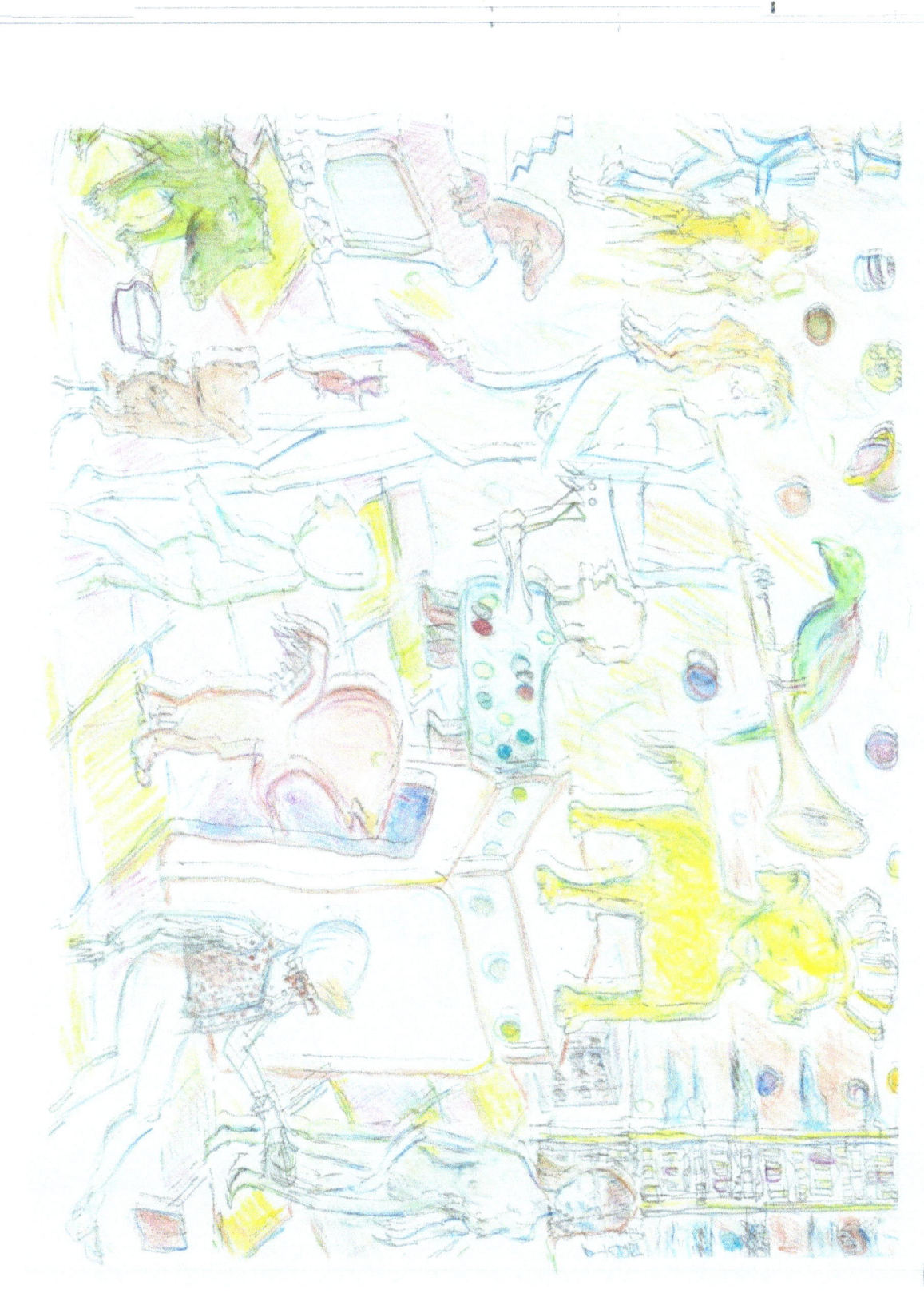

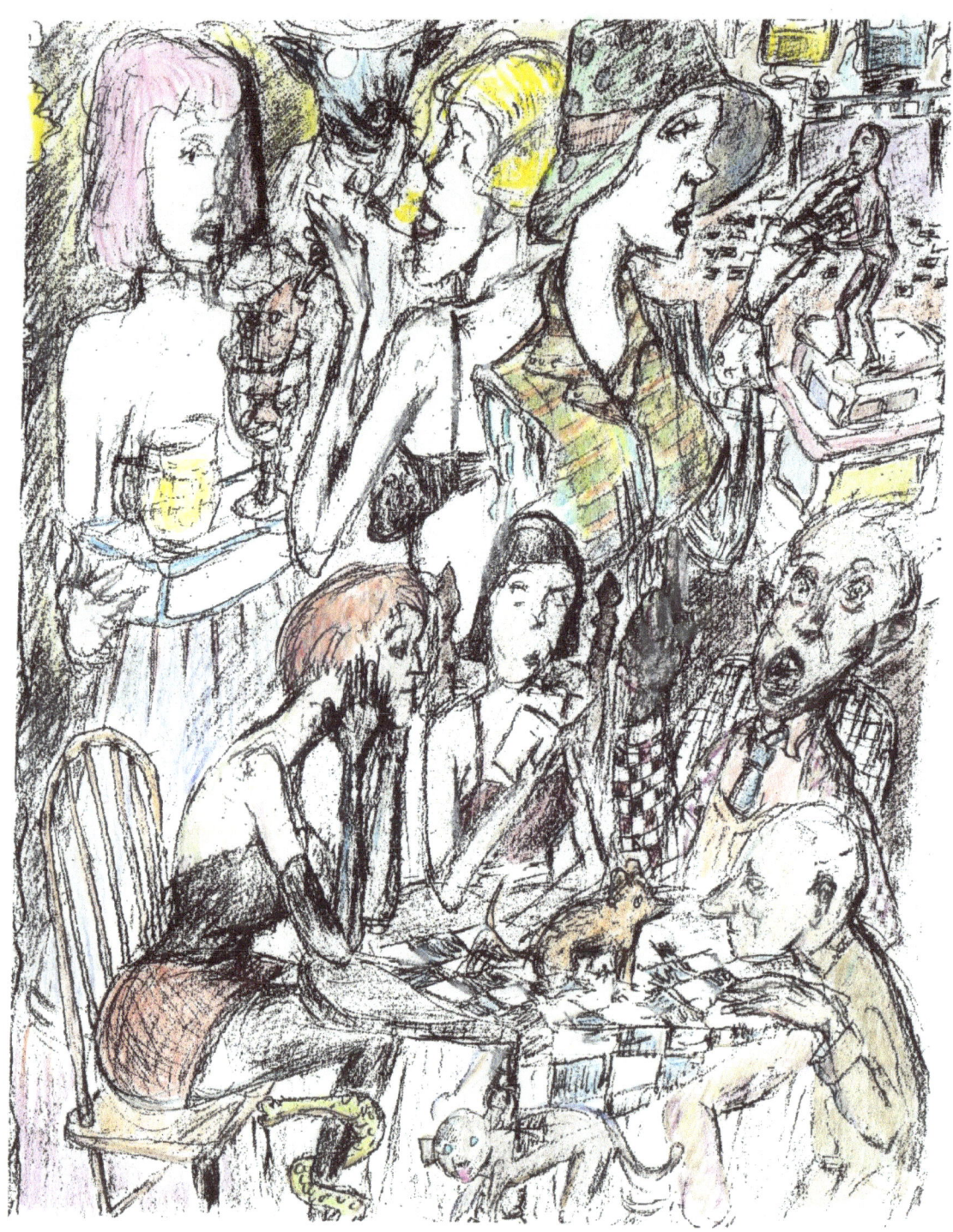

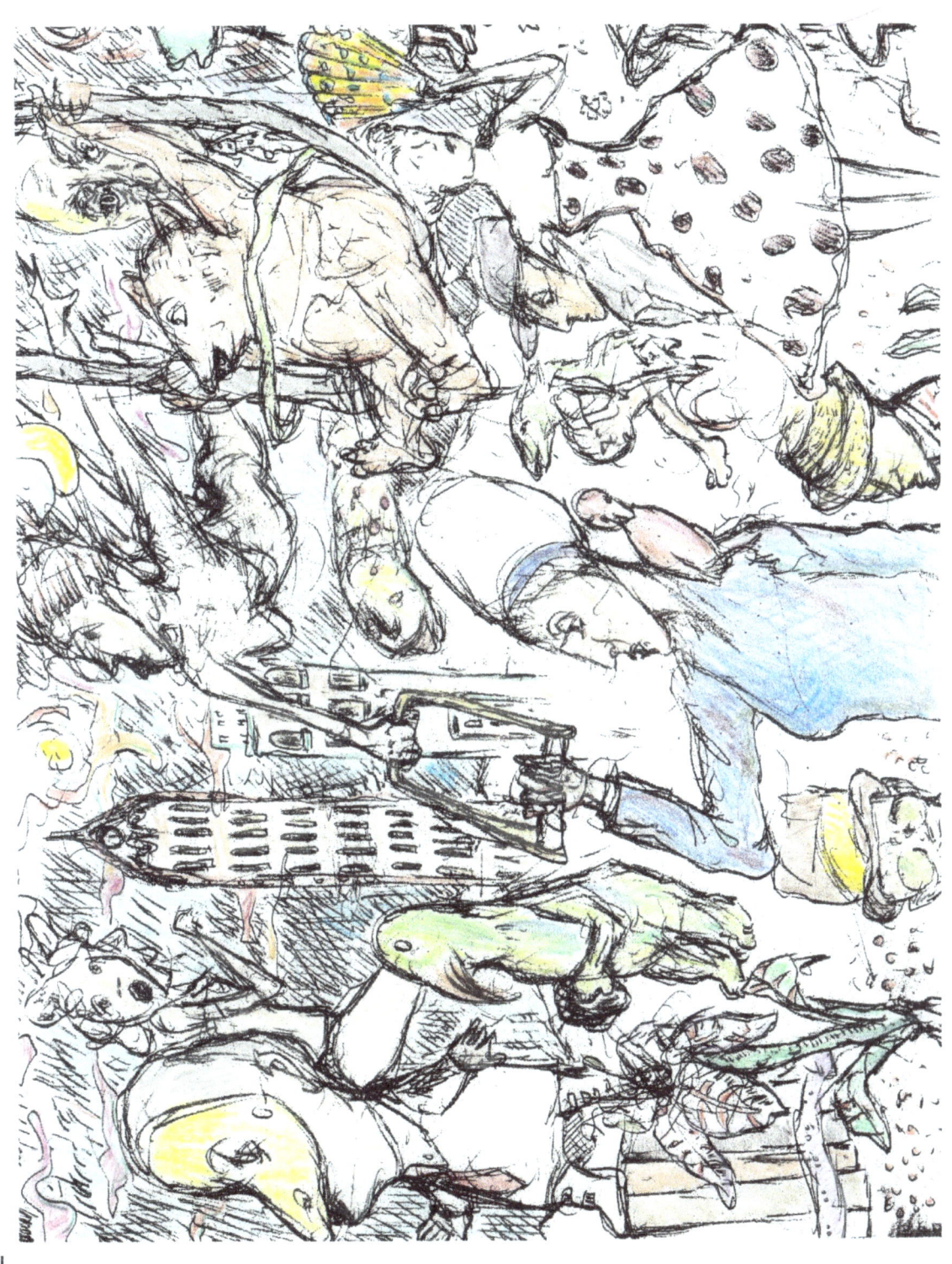

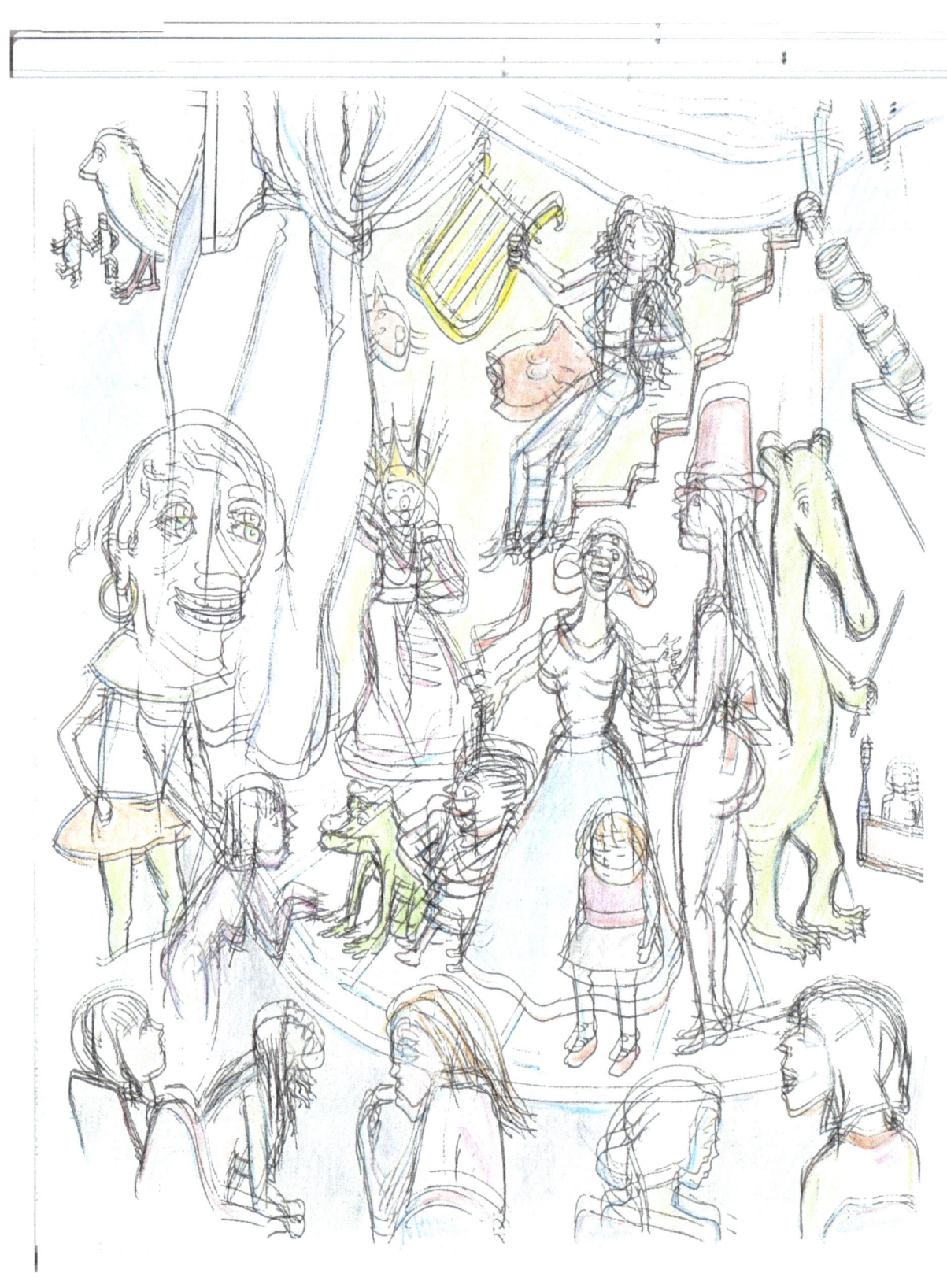

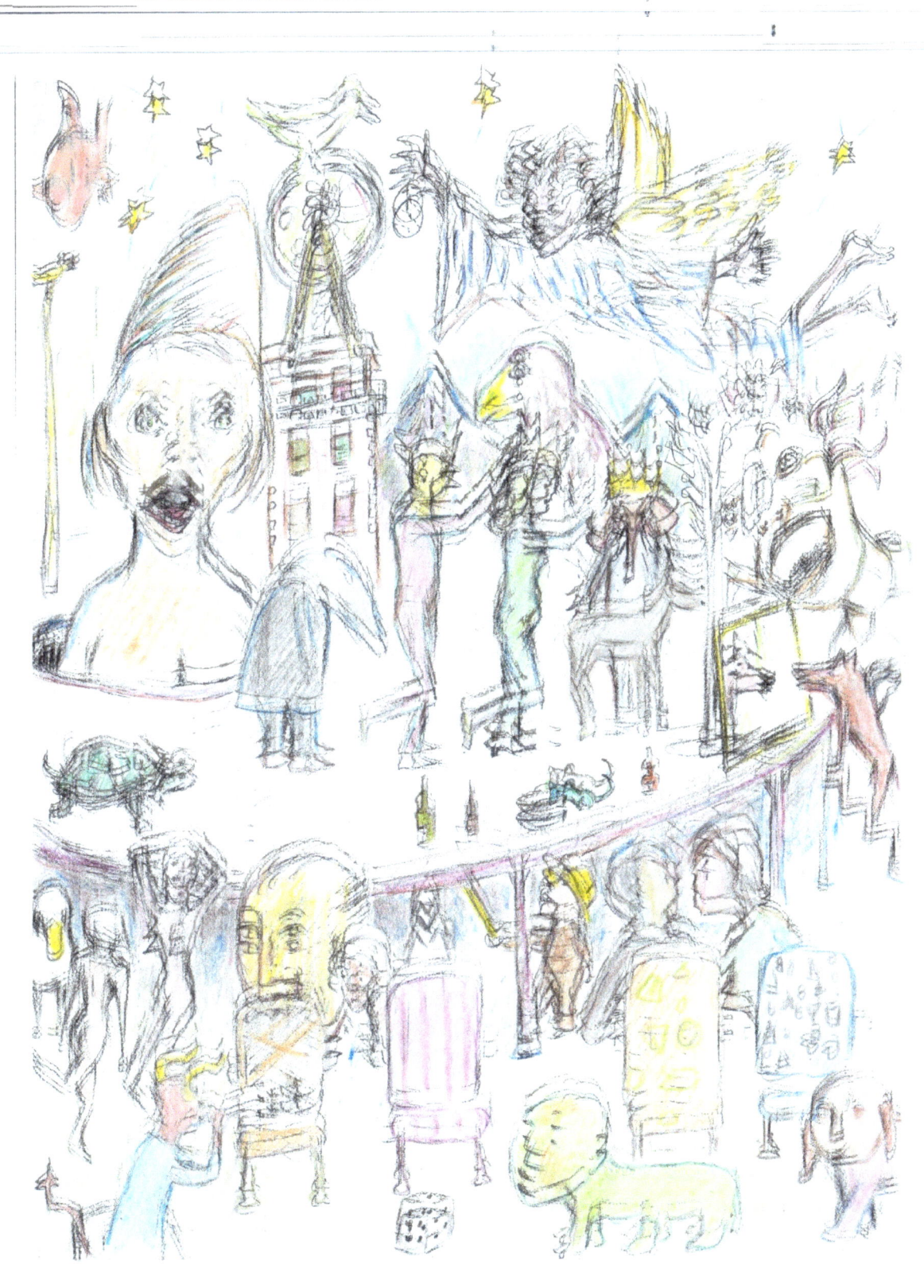

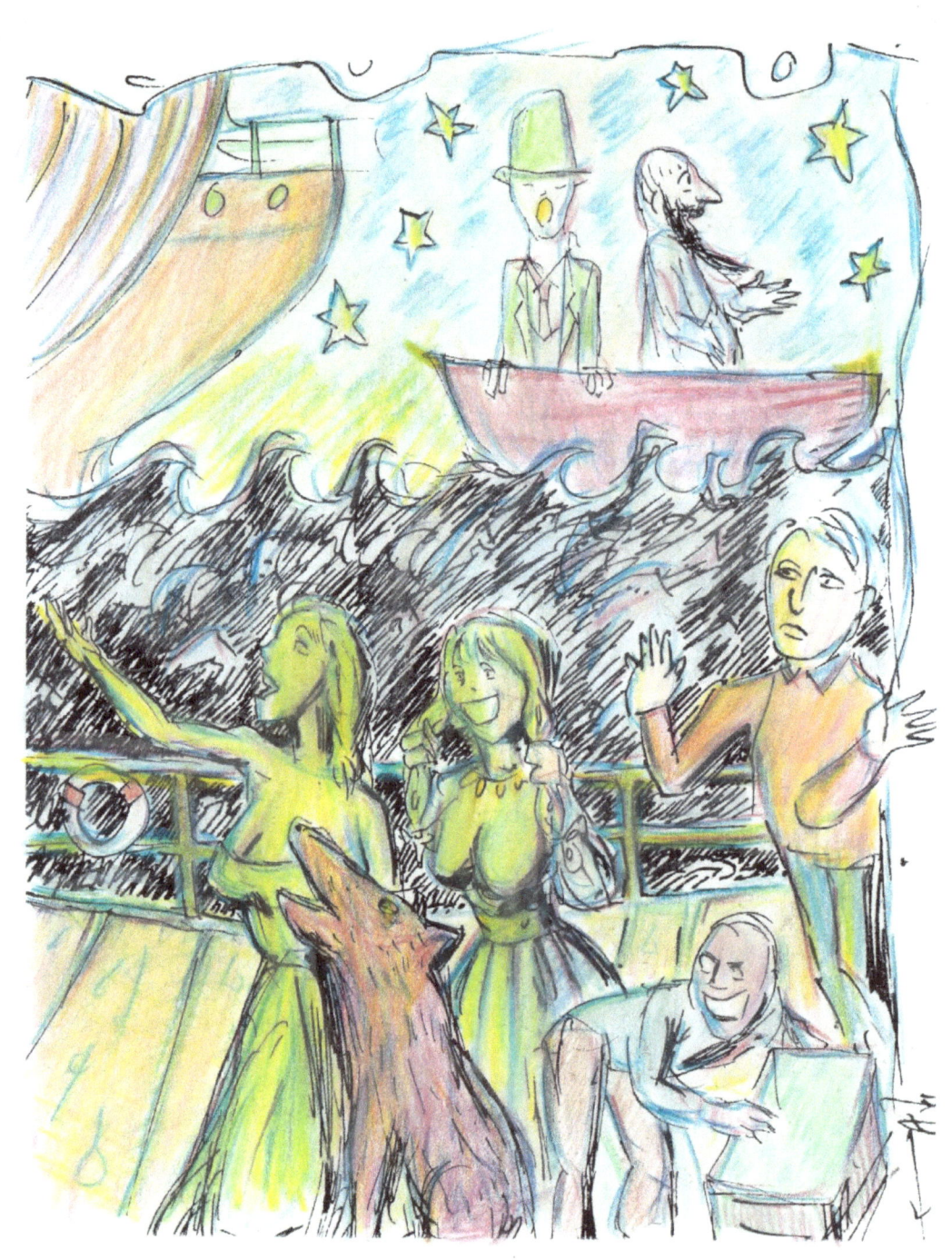

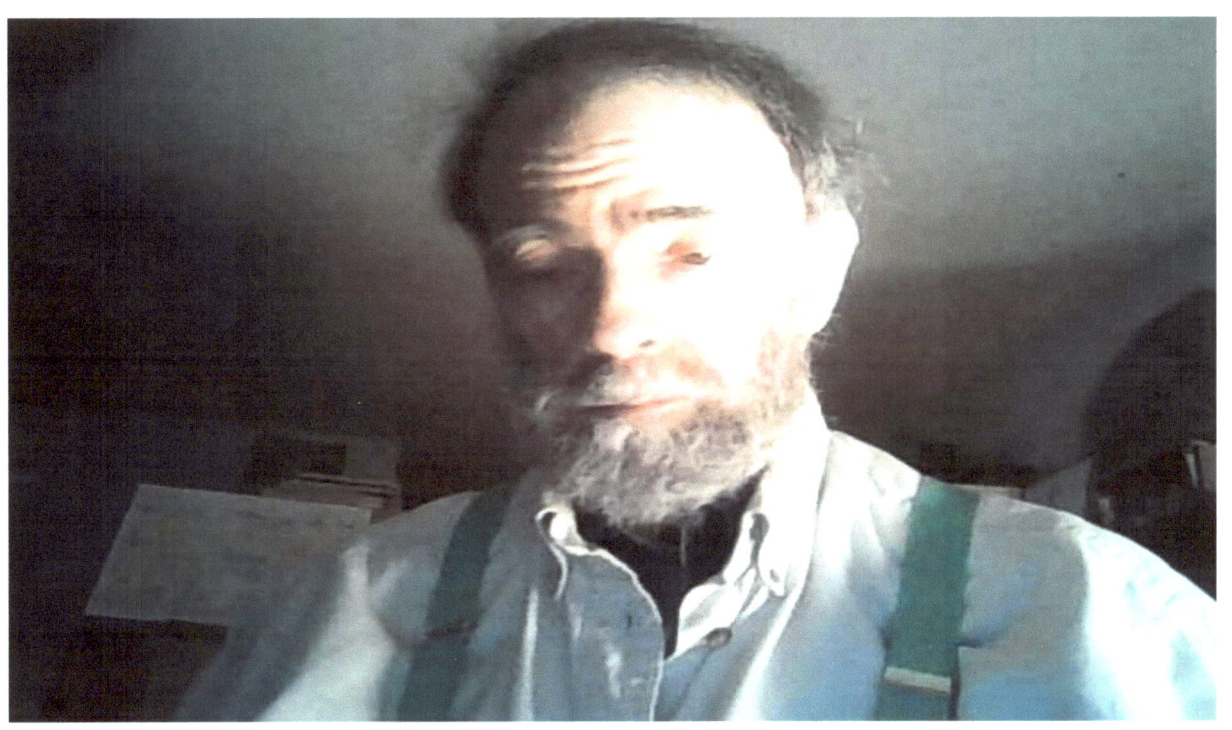

www.ingramcontent.com/pod-product-compliance
Lightning Source LLC
Chambersburg PA
CBHW051927210526
45473CB00006B/2157